COMMUNITY, COMPETITION AND
CITIZEN SCIENCE

Global Connections

Series Editor: Robert Holton, Trinity College, Dublin

Global Connections builds on the multi-dimensional and continuously expanding interest in Globalization. The main objective of the series is to focus on 'connectedness' and provide readable case studies across a broad range of areas such as social and cultural life, economic, political and technological activities.

The series aims to move beyond abstract generalities and stereotypes: 'Global' is considered in the broadest sense of the word, embracing connections between different nations, regions and localities, including activities that are trans-national, and trans-local in scope; 'Connections' refers to movements of people, ideas, resources, and all forms of communication as well as the opportunities and constraints faced in making, engaging with, and sometimes resisting globalization.

The series is interdisciplinary in focus and publishes monographs and collections of essays by new and established scholars. It fills a niche in the market for books that make the study of globalization more concrete and accessible.

Also published in this series:

Multiple Modernities and Postsecular Societies
Edited by Massimo Rosati and Kristina Stoeckl
ISBN 978-1-4094-4412-1

Legitimization in World Society
Edited by Aldo Mascareño and Kathya Araujo
ISBN 978-1-4094-4088-8

Global Islamophobia
Muslims and Moral Panic in the West
Edited by George Morgan and Scott Poynting
ISBN 978-1-4094-3119-0

Managing Cultural Change
Reclaiming Synchronicity in a Mobile World
Melissa Butcher
ISBN 978-1-4094-2510-6

Community, Competition and Citizen Science
Voluntary Distributed Computing in a Globalized World

ANNE HOLOHAN
Trinity College, Dublin, Ireland

Routledge
Taylor & Francis Group

LONDON AND NEW YORK

First published 2013 by Ashgate Publishing

Published 2016 by Routledge
2 Park Square, Milton Park, Abingdon, Oxfordshire OX14 4RN
711 Third Avenue, New York, NY 10017, USA

First issued in paperback 2016

Routledge is an imprint of the Taylor & Francis Group, an informa business

British Library Cataloguing in Publication Data
A catalogue record for this book is available from the British Library

The Library of Congress has cataloged the printed edition as follows:
Holohan, Anne, 1968-
    Community, competition and citizen science : voluntary distributed computing in a globalized world / by Anne Holohan.
        pages cm. -- (Global connections)
    Includes bibliographical references and index.
    ISBN 978-1-4094-5298-0 (hardback) 1. Volunteer workers in science. 2. Science-
-Social aspects. 3. Computer networks. 4. Information technology projects--Social aspects. I. Title.
    Q175.5.H64 2013
    303.48'34--dc23
                                                                                    2013009601

ISBN 13: 978-1-138-27186-9 (pbk)
ISBN 13: 978-1-4094-5298-0 (hbk)

Contents

List of Figures and Tables

Figures

Tables

Preface

Why is Voluntary Distributed Computing important for sociology? I think the answer lies in the word 'voluntary'; this is a scientific endeavour which is dependent on non-professionals offering their time and resources for a good cause. A good cause, incidentally, that can involve a lot of social activity. Many volunteers are members of a team, or a forum community, and many engage in vigorous competition, as each project has league tables of the most productive 'crunchers' of data, and these change on a daily basis. It is difficult to understand or work to recruit and retain those volunteers without using a sociological perspective. It is a truly global phenomenon and is having a significant impact on science everywhere but is also not widely known about. It was the fervour aroused by the competition in VDC among computer science graduate students/friends at UCLA that first alerted me to VDC back in 2000. Since then I have followed the activity of the group of projects featured in this book with a professional interest. As technology becomes ubiquitous and global in every field of human endeavour, sociology can contribute to a holistic understanding of the changes wrought and the possibilities offered.

Chapter 1

Introduction

In February 2011, two people found a new pulsar in space. One of those people, Vitaliy Shiryaev, was in Moscow. A man who has a PhD in radio astronomy, Shirayaev's day job is to solve what is called the 'travelling salesman problem': finding the shortest path between a cluster of cities for the trucks in the company, with the goal of saving a lot of money in fuel and time. In mathematical terms this is a nonpolynominal algorithm problem and requires Shiryaev to use a large computer cluster to get solutions. When his computer cluster is not busy solving the 'travelling salesman problem', he has them search for pulsars for the Einstein@home volunteer distributed computing project. Einstein@home searches gravitational wave data for signals from unknown pulsars. In February 2011, one of Shiryaev's computers found a radio pulsar orbiting a white dwarf star every 9.4 hours. The pulsar, called J1952+2630 was found coincidentally, independantly and simultaneously by an English man, Stacey Eastham. Like Shiryaev, Eastham has a day job. He is a motorcycle inspector for the British Ministry of Transport and it is in his spare time that he crunches data for Einstein@home on computers that he builds himself from recycled materials, including old water bottles.

Priscilla Burns is a retired school teacher in a small seaside town in the UK. Every morning, she gets up, goes to her computer and checks the message boards for ClimatePrediction.net (CPDN). This volunteer distributed computing project's aim is to explore how climate will change over the next century, by analyzing changes in levels of carbon dioxide amongst other measures. Burns is a moderator on the message boards, answering questions and making new volunteers feel welcome. She was a self-described 'non-techie' when she began her involvement by downloading the software onto her PC after watching a BBC news story on how ordinary citizens can participate in large scale scientific research. Five years into her involvement, she is now 'comfortable with computers', and is passionate about being part of the volunteer distributed computing community, enjoying the challenge of the interaction with the other people involved as much as her interaction with the technology and science.

Shiryaev, Eastham and Burns are part of a growing wave of individuals around the world, numbering in the millions, who voluntarily give their time and idle computer resources for scientific research. They are often referred to as 'volunteers', but just as often, as the main function is processing data, especially if they are less focused on the substance of what they are processing than on the competition to process the most, they refer to themselves as 'crunchers'. I will use both labels in this book.

So what are they volunteering/crunching on? A voluntary distributed computing (VDC) project like proving Einstein's theories or modelling climate change divides a big computational task into small pieces of data or work that are sent out over the Internet to be processed by individual users. These pieces are downloaded to personal computers, and the data is crunched when the computers are idle. Files are then uploaded to the servers that they originated from – with the completed computations – and the process starts over again. Millions of people all over the world are currently participating voluntarily in such projects. The amount of computing resources thus harnessed is enormous and would cost millions, if not billions, of dollars on the market. However, voluntary distributed computing only works if many people participate and continue to participate. The technical challenge is to manage large computing tasks by breaking them down to many small tasks, which are then allocated to a large number of individuals who volunteer their personal computers to the initiative. The social problem is how to find all those widely dispersed computers and persuade their owners to participate and to continue to participate. Two key questions need to be answered: What do we know about the factors driving participation in VDCs? How can a large scale scientific project provide an environment that would encourage resource contribution from many volunteers? And more fundamentally, what does VDC tell us about the impact of new technologies on collective action, community and science?

Background

The first step in considering these questions, and their answers, is to understand what makes VDC technically possible and why it's time has come. In the late 1990s and since, four phenomena have come together to permit the technical or computational challenge to be met; two phenomena in the everyday world and two in the computer science and academic world.

1) In computer science, distributed computing was developed as an efficient way to perform extensive calculations quickly. Even before the widespread availability of local networks, data processing tasks could manually be assigned to different individual computers by assigning different data files, cards or tapes to them. The widespread deployment of local networks at research universities in the late 1970s and early 1980s (Metcalf and Boggs, 1976; Roberts, 1986) allowed automation of this form of distribution computation and the establishment of the field of distributed computing as a branch of computer science (Korpela, 2012).

2) The second phenomenon is the increasingly central role computation plays in all scientific research, from biology to physics to biochemistry to genetics, and hence the rise of huge demand for very powerful 'supercomputers', capable of processing enormous amounts of data. A supercomputer is a computer designed to do large-scale and complicated computation by 'parallelizing' it – to divide it into pieces that can be worked on by separate processors at the same time. Most modern supercomputers work this way, using many processors in one box

(Yao, 2006; Anderson, 2003). Voluntary Distributed Computing uses the Internet to connect computers worldwide, to create a virtual supercomputer. Indeed, today the majority of the world's computing power is no longer in supercomputer centres and institutional machine rooms, but in billions of personal computers and game consoles all over the world.

3) There has been a vast increase in the number of computers connected to the Internet at least part of the time. Starting in the early 1990s, the Internet began to evolve from a government owned network of computers located at universities, research institutions, government agencies, and computer hardware manufacturers to a network available to all individuals and businesses operated in privately held infrastructure. This evolution led to a huge increase in the number of computers, both in businesses and in homes, that were connected to the Internet at least part of the time.

4) Personal Computers (PCs), portable computers, and more recently handheld devices have became faster. The technology industry responded to the huge emerging market for PCs by investing in innovation. They were willing to spend more to develop a Central Processing Unit (CPU) chip if it was going to sell a million of them. So the chips used in home computers (e.g. the Intel Pentium) have developed so quickly that they double in speed about every 18 months, the so-called Moore's Law. The rate of progress is even faster for 'graphics coprocessors', the chips that handle 3D graphics in PCs and game consoles. Their doubling time is about eight months and they are programmable and flexible. Most computational tasks require storage (disk space) as well as computing. Again, the typical PC in 2005 provided about 80 gigabytes of storage capacity which has increased to an average of 500 gigabytes of storage capacity in 2012, most of which is not used by the PC owner. The net effect of these developments is that PCs have become very fast – as fast as supercomputers only a few years older. Yet the normal activities for which a PC is used – surfing the Internet, checking e-mail, using Word and Excel – barely dents the potential of a modern processor that can operate at many hundreds of million instructions per second. Most of the time, the processor sits idle, waiting for something to do and while sitting there performs a special operation that does nothing, hence why the cycle is called an idle cycle. Suddenly, there were millions if not over a billion, fast computers connected by a network all with an enormous number of idle cycles to spare (Anderson, 2003; Korpela, 2012).

In the mid-1990s, all that was needed to harness the implications of these four developments was a mechanism to connect the individual computers with a project. Voluntary Distributed Computing is that mechanism. It is straightforward: large computing tasks are first broken into much smaller tasks (often called Work Units or WUs), which are then sent over the Internet to lots of smaller computers for processing. These smaller work units are then processed utilizing only the unused computing cycles or idle cycles. When a work unit is completely processed, the result is then uploaded to a central server which has the responsibility of storing the results and doing any post-processing if necessary. The central server sorts and arranges the data received in such a way that the processed data points combine in order to effectively function as if the entire problem was processed in one extremely powerful supercomputer.

In 1995–96, several individuals and groups simultaneously but independently recognized the ability to use distributed computing outside of academic networks, and thus build projects larger than several hundred machines by recruiting volunteers. The first large-scale projects to do this and gain public appeal were prime number hunting by the Great Internet Mersenne Prime Search (GIMPS) and encryption cracking efforts by Distributed.net (Beberg et al., 2009). They appeared as the public began to access the Internet. A second wave of projects began in 1999 with SETI@home which searches for signs of intelligent extraterrestrial life in radio signals, and Folding@home, which researches how proteins, RNA, and nanoscale synthetic polymers fold, thus giving insight to causes of diseases. During this wave, voluntary distributed computing took off in popularity, and by 2012 there were hundreds of active Voluntary Distributed Computing projects with a wide range of sizes and goals.

The infrastructure necessary for VDC must handle the distribution of software and Work Units to users worldwide, the web pages they will see for their work statistics and the network communication between the users and project servers. In the early days of VDC, this required about two years of work for two full-time software engineers (Christensen, 2005). The early projects – GIMPS, SETI, and Distributed.net – all ran their own architecture, with significant drawbacks: projects had to either maintain executables for every platform they wished to support or provide source code so that the volunteers could port and compile their own applications. More significantly, the scientists designing the code were often not experts in the concepts of TCP/IP (transmission control/internet protocol) networking, resulting in servers that were more vulnerable to server congestion, denial of service and other attacks (Korpela, 2012).

A framework that combined all these tasks and could be used for any project was developed and launched in 2003 in Berkeley by David Anderson, one of the founders of SETI@home project and he called it the BOINC project, the Berkeley Open Infrastructure for Network Computing. Today, most VDC projects 'live' at or use BOINC, but there are notable exceptions which still go their own way, such as GIMPS.

What must the owner of the PC who wants to engage in VDC do? In the early days of VDC, the participants downloaded the software directly from the website of the project they were interested in, onto their computer. This software not only handles information queries, storage management, and processing scheduling, but also does authentication and data encryption to ensure information security (Yao, 2006). The software application is designed to run continuously at low priority or to wait until the computer is not in use either by watching for keyboard/mouse activity or by running as a screensaver (Korpela, 2012).

The cost is minimal to the volunteer with the PC. VDC allows scientists to tackle scientific calculations that they could not otherwise do for reasons of cost, space, overhead and operational complexity (Beberg et al., 2009). The costs of local computation – the hardware, electricity, cooling, floor space and system administrators – are greatly reduced if not eliminated. The cost of the volunteer's computer and the Internet connection is already spent since they need a computer for other reasons. This makes the only additional cost the difference in electrical use of the busy system versus an idle system. This per-volunteer cost has been considered insignificant by the volunteers, but may become a concern if electrical costs increase greatly. As volunteers upgrade their computers for other reasons, the capacity of the project increases as a result, an inbuilt 'Moore's Law' effect.

The individuals involved in VDC are an essential part of its success and in understanding how the field of citizen scientific research has developed. David Anderson is a key figure in Voluntary Distributed Computing, described by one respondent as 'the Godfather of VDC', and is held in enormous respect throughout the VDC community. As with many VDC-ers, he had a childhood passion for mathematics and computers, and at the time he was involved with the launch of SETI he was a Professor in Computer Science at the University of California, Berkeley. He was always interested in distributed computing but what triggered the idea was discussions with a then graduate student about the 25th anniversary of the Apollo Moon Landing in 1995. He says,

> The Apollo Project galvanized the American public with respect to science for the 10 years leading up to the Landing and there was a lot of excitement about space travel and science. More people began going into engineering fields but then it all subsided. We began thinking about what could we do now to get the public in large numbers thinking about science again. That period around 1995 was a time when consumers were getting onto the Internet in large numbers and PCs were actually powerful enough to do significant scientific computations for the first time.

After getting funding from the National Science Foundation and starting SETI he continues,

> I started thinking about the potential of that approach to other areas of science. From the beginning I was not interested specifically in SETI but more in the general idea of aggregating public computing power and sort of any kind of occupational science project.

He began work on what was to become BOINC, the middleware which provides a platform to easily create new projects. Although BOINC has been a huge success, it still only represents, he estimates,

> 1 per cent of the total potential. I'd really like to see volunteer distributed computing getting used by essentially all scientists. It's an easy one that doesn't require extra work for them.

One of the challenges to overcome in order for this goal to be realized is the discomfort many scientists have with the uncertainty of working with volunteers. The people behind the computers are not as controllable as a computer cluster in the scientist's own building. There is no guarantee that the volunteers are not all going to disappear. This has not happened in any of the big projects which are very strong but it touches upon the key non-technical challenge of VDC: how do you recruit and retain participants?

Data and Methods for Understanding the Social Challenge

As technology becomes ubiquitous and global in every field of human endeavour, sociology can contribute to a holistic understanding of the changes wrought and the possibilities afforded. The social processes in VDC reflect how social forces will work in the future and VDC offers us a case study through which we can gain a greater understanding of the social changes happening in all fields of human action. Nov et al. observed, 'while the computational aspects of volunteer [distributed] computing [has] received much research attention, the participative aspect remains largely unexplored' (Nov et al., 2010: 741). The most significant advantage and greatest complexity of any volunteer distributed computing initiative is the reliance on volunteers to set up and run clients (project software on PCs), and to continue running them.

   Recruitment is a constant issue and getting the word out to the public about any particular project remains a great challenge. The best hope for Voluntary Distributed Computing projects is that the project itself has great public appeal. Marketing and public relations can help, as well as publications of news and results in the scientific literature and major media outlets. For BOINC projects, mention on the main BOINC website or other volunteer computing project websites or user websites can be a big help in attracting followers. The online survey for this book in 2010 and 2011 showed that Internet sources were the primary means by which volunteers first encounter specific projects.

   So once the word about a particular project has reached their ears or eyes, who are the volunteers and why do they volunteer their time and computers in voluntary distributed computing? Why do people volunteer resources for the collective good? There are three main areas of motivation identified thus far in the literature: science, competition and community (Nov et al., 2010; Holohan and Garg, 2005; Krebs, 2010; Darch and Carusi, 2011). Regardless of the particular motivation of volunteers, it is clear that the Internet has opened up public or citizen science in unprecedented ways. Chapter 2 profiles the key projects which are the focus of this book. In Chapter 3, I explore the implications VDC has for the institution of science, from a practical and a sociological theory perspective? In light of VDC, who can be considered a scientist? What does the practice of science mean today? What is a research community? How is research conducted differently today than it was 25 years ago?

In Chapter 4, I explore our evolving understanding of the theory and practice of communities in light of the changes and possibilities wrought by the internet and new forms of connectedness. The intense nourishing of small sub-communities of the larger project communities has the richest dividend in terms of social support, learning and project longevity. These communities are based in forums which have their own internal structure and dynamic. The forums offer users both technical support and a sense of community and are a very good source of feedback for the project. Each project has a website that is the central location for all of the information and includes news, answers to frequently answered questions, results and papers. I will discuss how community is experienced through VDC and feature a case study of a particularly lively VDC forum, the Mersenne Forum, which supports GIMPS.

One way volunteers are motivated is through competition and gaming which is the focus of Chapter 5. Competition has been and remains a driving force in VDC with many volunteers explicitly in it for the spirit of competition and achievement in outperforming other crunchers. The user statistic website is central to any VDC project because it allows volunteers to see how much they are contributing, and they can compare themselves to all other crunchers. Every project has a large database storing every result received and the credits (points) assigned to each user and team. Log files from the server are gathered up periodically and the completed work is credited to the volunteer and team for public display. Volunteers compete against each other individually and in teams with the credits assigned for completing work units. Some volunteers are fiercely loyal to a particular project while at the same time being intensely competitive, while others are indifferent to the project or projects they are working on, it is the credits they care about. In an effort to boost their statistics, they often upgrade their hardware more aggressively than those not involved in VDC. I feature a case study of Team Lamb Chop, one particularly successful team, and the tactics it employed. The irony of it is, just as it has always been for scientific research, that although the process is competitive, collaboration with other people, through VDC Teams, increases the likelihood of success, and the meaning of the success is enhanced by the approbation received on the many forums set up to facilitate discussion of all things VDC for the projects. Peer presence and potential sanction/exclusion also helps ensure ethical behaviour.

There is a variety of roles within the social ecosystem that is VDC. The people involved in VDC are not just the volunteers: the scientists and the computer programmers or system administrators play a key role in both the recruitment and retention of participants. The volunteers themselves are not a monolithic body: an intermediate layer between the paid people on the project (the scientists and programmers) and the unpaid volunteers is the 'specialist' core of volunteers: the moderators, the beta testers and the language volunteers. Chapter 6 will explore the role of moderators in more detail and show how they are an underappreciated but essential 'bridge' between the top of the project and the mass of volunteers. Chapter 7 will explain the role of system administrators and the scientists themselves, who vary both in terms of how they understand and use VDC, in particular their relationship with the volunteers, with implications for the success and longevity of the project. In Chapter 8, I show that the mass of volunteers are not as mixed a bag as one might expect: the vast majority of volunteers are male and many of those are self-confessed 'techies'. I will examine the motivation and roles of the volunteers overall, and also explore the experience of women and non-techies in the projects, teams and forums. Chapter 9 concludes with a review of why VDC is important to look at sociologically and what sociology can contribute to our understanding of how it works and why it matters. I will look at the future of VDC, and assess the factors that will take VDC down a number of potential paths. All of this is set in the context of the experience of volunteers in a number of projects, with data from an online survey of 200 VDC volunteers from a variety of projects conducted in late 2010 and early 2011. During 2011 and 2012, I also conducted 20 in-depth interviews with volunteers, moderators, system administrators and scientists from several projects. I conducted ethnographic (online) fieldwork, principally observation, in the forums of GIMPS, Folding@ home, SETI@home, and ClimatePrediction.net during this period. I base the insights and analytic points made in this book on the data yielded from using these three methods.

The Sociological Contribution

So why does this all matter from a social perspective? A key factor is that the volunteers do this for free, no money changes hands, and no expenses are reimbursed. The same processes that enabled VDC have produced a communications environment built on cheap processors with high computation abilities, interconnected in a pervasive network, the Internet. This combined with a shift, in the advanced economies of the world, to an economy centred on information (financial services, software, science), cultural production (films, music) and the manipulation of symbols (branded goods manufactured elsewhere) has brought an unprecedented capability for individual and social production of information (Benkler, 2007). The material means of information production (and cultural production) is now in the hands of individuals, and these networked individuals comprise a significant fraction of the world's population. When these networked individuals cooperate together they can, in effect, establish a new mode of production, a social production of information, where individuals can produce, coordinate and disseminate information at little or no cost beyond the cost of the PC they are working on. Networks have joined groups and hierarchies as social and organization models (Castells, 1996). The physical barriers of cost and equipment, the necessary capital that characterized the industrial mode of production, are no longer barriers. In the industrial economy, but not the networked information economy, the practical individual freedom to cooperate with others in making things of value has been limited by the extent of the capital requirements of production. 'Specifically, new and important cooperative and coordinate action carried out through radically distributed, nonmarket mechanisms that do not depend on proprietary strategies – play a much greater role than it did or could have in the industrial information economy' (Benkler, ibid.).

All the inputs necessary for effective productive capacity are under the control of individual users. The majority of individuals have the threshold level of material capacity required to explore the information environment, to occupy it, to take from it, and to make their own contributions to it. People have bought their PCs and once used for earnings-generation activity, the excess capacity is there to be used. This has enabled the emergence of effective, large-scale cooperative peer production of information, knowledge and culture such as VDC and the Open-Source Movement. The core characteristics underlying the success of these are their modularity – they can broken into small pieces – and their capacity to integrate many fine grained contributions.

Because the two modes of production, industrial and social, are woven together, but have no market or in-firm organization to connect them, collaboration is important. VDC is an entirely voluntary, collaborative endeavour. A project with only one volunteer will not succeed. So there is at one level the collaboration between the volunteers themselves, and at another, the collaboration between these actors in the networked information economy and the actors who are straddling both the networked information economy and the industrial economy, the scientists. Our knowledge of collaboration in this area is scanty and needs empirical investigation.

This book is a case study of the field of Voluntary Distributed Computing, the 'networked individuals': (Rainie and Wellman, 2012) that make it possible, and how it works in practice. It is also a study of the individuals who are part of the proprietary strategies still dominant in scientific research – the scientists and programmers and funders of VDC – who are straddling the old industrial economy way of doing research and the new networked information economy of social production of information. VDC is a case-study of the networked individual, working outside the market, to produce information and knowledge that is as valuable as that produced by the traditional, proprietary state and industrial titans. In the VDC case, that would be the supercomputers, the scientists, and the research institution, the cost of accessing which was prohibitive under the conditions of the industrial economy. The networked information economy does not exist independently of and 'outside' the industrial economy but the two are weaving together in ways that merit examination. In VDC, funding mostly comes from the state, the scientists are mostly part of research institutions and the hardware is proprietary hardware. The volunteers, the moderators, the software and the information produced, however, are that of the networked information economy. One of the reasons BOINC was set up was precisely that the desire to run a VDC around a particular project was not enough. David Anderson explains,

> You need to have software expertise, you need to know something about public relations. You need to run your own servers. You need to be available 24 hours a day. It adds up to a combination of skills that the average biologist even if he or she is a computational biologist doesn't have.

Benkler (ibid.) pointed out that the empowered individual and the social production of information threatens the incumbents of the industrial information economy, as it questions the values on which their institutions were built. David Anderson of BOINC put the opposition to VDC of a large part of the scientific establishment thus:

> It's one of those where the reaction is not completely rational and you have to sort of decipher it. I think the biggest factor is one of ownership and control. Many scientists like to have their computers in a locked room and they like to own them. The more money they cost in a way the more powerful they are. They have their little kingdoms and their empires. The thing with Volunteer Distributed Computing is you don't own anything. You get computer power only by appealing to the public and doing things like making educational web pages and running message boards and things like that, well outside the expertise of scientists' IT people. And you don't need a million dollar budget to do it.

Such resistant views reflect and represent a hierarchical structure and view which is under tremendous pressure. As Tapscott and Williams (2007: 1–3) put it in *Wikinomics*,

> While hierarchies are not vanishing, profound changes in the nature of technology, demographics, and the global economy are giving rise to powerful new models of production based on community, collaboration, and self-organization rather than on hierarchy and control...This is more than open source, social networking, so called crowd sourcing, smart mobs, crowd wisdom, or other ideas that touch upon the subject.

They argue that there is an institutional crisis in business, education, science, media and government as the industrial economy which worked so well for a significant period of time is now stalling and unable to cope with the need for sustainable development in a world where billions in the emerging economy want the same middle class lifestyle as they see in the West.

'Leisure capital' is the time and cognitive and interest surplus that people have, and this combined with the interconnectedness leads to growing resources in society that can be deployed in a wide variety of ways. Clay Shirkey (2010) coined the phrase 'cognitive surplus' to describe our society's disposable time and energy – all the time we collectively have when we are not dealing with the basic obligations of life, such as making a living and feeding our family. It is the time put into leisure activities such as watching television, or going out with friends, or relaxing with a hobby. Mostly, these activities are done alone or in small groups. What the online tools do is make it easy to coordinate complex creative projects in a large group. VDC is one example of a clever way to connect laypeople to make contributions to a field of human endeavour, in this instance science. Many more people are clever enough and motivated to contribute to and engage in science than the industrial communications infrastructure allowed.

The focus on the institutions is important as it provides analytical traction on what is happening. Institutions are rules and shared meanings that define social relationships, help define who occupies what position in these relationships, and guide interaction by giving actors cognitive frames or sets of meanings to interpret the behaviour of others. Action is constrained not only by structural position but also by the organization's cognitive and normative orientation (Meyer, Scott and Deal, 1981; Powell and DiMaggio 1983). New Institutionalist theories concern how fields of action[1] come into existence, remain stable and can be transformed. While an organizational practice may have its origins in certain rational principles, it can become institutionalized over time and continue to be used even though it may no longer be beneficial to the organization (Zucker, 1977; 1987; 1989; Roy, 1997; Fligstein, 1985; 1990).[2] In turbulent times or environments, rules can be made from laws in intended or unintended ways and/or can be borrowed from other fields to create new institutions. Individuals with appropriate social skills can create new social orders or 'fields' through their ability to get others to cooperate with them (Fligstein, 2001).

David Anderson of SETI@home and BOINC, Bruce Allen of Einstein@home, George Woltman at GIMPS, the system administrators who work 'Silicon Valley hours for academic pay' and the moderators who volunteer huge amounts of time on a daily basis, they are the leaders in offering one new way of doing large-scale science. In doing so, they are helping transform the field or institution of science and the organizations and behaviour of those within it. Fligstein (ibid.) observed that such social actors with the appropriate skills for transforming fields of endeavour at a time of technological change have an usually powerful and transformative

---

1 'Fields' or 'arenas' or 'games' are local social orders. Fields (Bourdieu 1977; Bourdieu and Wacquant, 1992) refer to situations where organized groups of actors gather and frame their actions vis-à-vis one another.

2 The institutional claim that social and cultural pressures lead to organized conformity builds on philosophical underpinnings of German idealists and phenomenologists most clearly represented in the writings of Berger and Luckmann (1967). Social reality is a human construct and a by-product of repetitive interactions. Thus organizational activities become institutionalized, taking the form of 'rationalized myths' when repeated over a period of time (Meyer and Rowan, 1977). The idea that the formal structure may be embraced as myth and ceremony in order to signal legitimacy lies at the very heart of the new institutional perspective. Indeed, once a threshold of firms adopt an innovation, most future adoption, especially in an uncertain environment, is more likely to result from mimetic, coercive or normative isomorphism than from competition (DiMaggio and Powell, 1981).

role to play. It is only in technological times of flux that transformations of fields are possible.

The structure of the VDC community reflects the networked information economy. Not all groups in a global network such as the VDC community are all equally connected. All connections and links form the pattern of a network and much can be learned from uncovering and observing the structure of a network. As Barabasi (2003) observed in his study of links on the Internet, far from everything being connected equally, there are hubs in a network to which most nodes are connected. Information, data, disease, gossip – they all travel through hubs in networks, and this network pattern is evident throughout nature and throughout human behaviour, once we know how and where to look (Watts 2004; Barabasi, ibid.). Taking a closer look at the hubs in VDC reveals much of the institutional rules and norms that are emerging from this endeavour. The projects, the forums, the individuals – the hubs into which almost all others are connected play a very powerful role and merit closer investigation. VDC is closely linked to the Open-Source movement in that a lot of people are contributing their time and skill for no remuneration, in a spirit of community. The Internet allowed this sharing to happen on a global scale in a way that had not been possible before.

In short, there two ways in which VDC is important: firstly, it is a demonstration of a new form of production of information based on individuals sharing their time and expertise on a global scale, and secondly, this new form of production has had an enormous impact on the established field of scientific research.

Chapter 2
The Projects

From the early days in the early 1990s, the Voluntary Distributed Computing world has expanded from a handful of small projects to a situation where there are hundreds of Voluntary Distributed Computing projects across a vast array of topics. Just what kind of project is suitable for VDC? The answer is that computationally heavy projects in most fields of science are suitable, as is demonstrated by the sample of projects I discuss here. Most VDC projects can be classified in one of four broad categories. There are also a number of esoteric projects or projects that do not fall into the four categories below and I include them in a fifth 'catch-all' category. The BOINC platform is not a project, but was the catalyst for the enormous growth in the number and variety of projects out there and is 'home' for most of the VDC projects. Because of its significance, I also discuss its development and role in the VDC. The projects I discuss here fall into one of the following five categories:

1. Mathematical projects
2. Physics and astronomy projects
3. Biological sciences projects.
4. Earth science projects
5. Catch-all

1. Mathematical Projects

Mathematical projects do numbers related projects such as searching for prime numbers of specific types or trying to solve cryptography problems.

GIMPS http://www.mersenne.org/

One of the first widespread distributed computing projects was the Great Internet Mersenne Primes Search (GIMPS) that started in late 1995. GIMPS is one of the longest lasting and greatest loyalty-inspiring VDC projects. This has been achieved through the interaction of the individuals involved and the priorities embedded in that interaction, producing a robust institution dedicated to mathematical knowledge and the like-minded people who constitute it. The objective of this project is to do a systematic search to find new Mersenne primes that invariably happen to be very large prime numbers as well. Finding extremely large primes had mostly been the preserve of people with access to fast (and expensive) supercomputers until GIMPS started. In fact, almost all of the 22 Mersenne primes found from 1952 to 1996 were found using supercomputers. Within a year of GIMPS' arrival this changed and 14 Mersenne primes found since then (the largest known primes at this time) have been found by GIMPS participants using consumer hardware such as ordinary desktop computers. The project initially started by distributing work via email to about 30 participants using Pentium 90s. It later graduated to using a server for automatically assigning work to participants over the Internet and now boasts some 97,000 participants using over 71,000 machines (late 2012).

A Mersenne prime is a prime of the form 2^P-1. The first Mersenne primes are 3, 7, 31, 127. An integer greater than one is called a prime number if its only divisors are one and itself. Mersenne primes have been central to number theory since they were first discussed by Euclid in 350 BC. The Fundamental Theorem of Arithmetic says they are the building blocks of numbers. From an applied perspective, primes are important to encryption and could lead to uncrackable codes. So-called higher 'Mersenne' prime numbers are named after the seventeenth century French mathematician Marin Mersenne, a seventeenth century French monk who first studied the rare numbers 300 years ago. He made a prediction about which values of 'P' would yield a prime. It took 300 years and many important discoveries in mathematics to prove his conjecture. It took VDC to accelerate the process.

When George Woltman began the project, he never expected such interest in number theory from people all over the world. A self-described 'math and computer geek', he is an early-retired computer engineer whose favourite thing in the world is to write programmes and study numbers. In 1995, he wrote a programme, in Assembly language, one of the most difficult programming languages, which checked for Mersenne Prime Numbers, uploaded it to the web and responded to queries via email. In 1998, a man called Scott in San Diego emailed Woltman and offered to host the GIMPS project on a server, thus enabling automatic downloading and uploading for the project. In 2003, Mike Vang in North Carolina offered to start a forum to replace the email list, and so the Mersenne Forum was born, and has generated very high loyalty and longevity among the many GIMPSers who have joined it. Woltman has never met either Scott or Mike, but together they continue to host a project, in Woltman's words, 'for people who love numbers'.

Apart from adding to mathematical knowledge, GIMPS has turned out to be excellent for testing computer hardware. The free Gimps program has identified hidden hardware problems in many computers.

In 2008, The Electronic Frontier Foundation awarded GIMPS the $100,000 Cooperative Computing Award for the August 23rd discovery of the 45th known Mersenne prime ('M45') 243,112,609-1, a mammoth 12,978,189 digit number, found on a University of California Los Angeles (UCLA) computer in the GIMPS PrimeNet network, after GIMPS met every requirement for the award for discovery of the first 10 million-digit prime number. Professor Edson Smith and the Maths Department received $50,000, charity got $25,000 and 25,000 was used primarily to fund more prime discoveries. In May 2000, a previous participant won the foundation's $50,000 award for discovering the first million-digit prime.

Every so often, such media coverage of a new Mersenne draws attention once again to one of the longest established and most loyally followed projects. Yet the vast majority of contributors will never hit the headlines; hundreds of thousands of individuals using their home computer and free software as part of an international grid of networked computers, search daily for new Mersenne Prime Numbers. A much smaller number of maths enthusiasts and subset of the crunchers come together on the Mersenne forum to brainstorm and hang out with like minded people. This community is the hub of the project and provides the interactional 'glue' which gives the project its distinctive culture.

2. Physics and Astronomy projects

SETI@home http://setiathome.berkeley.edu

I now turn to a project which is one of the most successful in harnessing the competitive element in individual volunteer's motivation. It has combined individual efforts and collective efforts through teams, all of whom compete publicly and vigorously. But the overall winner of this competition is the project and scientific research. Also the most famous Voluntary Distributed Computing Project, SETI@home (SETI stands for the 'Search for Extra-Terrestrial Intelligence') originated at the University of California, Berkeley in May 1999. SETI@home is a scientific experiment that uses Internet-connected computers in the Search for Extraterrestrial Intelligence (SETI). A project of the University of California Space Sciences laboratory, SETI@home was one of the earliest large VDCs. The primary purpose of SETI is to analyze radio telescope data recorded at the National Astronomy and Ionosphere Center's Arecibo Observatory in Puerto Rico, and more recently, the National Radio Astronomy Observatory's Green Bank Observatory in West Virginia.

The project did indeed capture the public imagination, and has been enormously successful, with over 5 million users at its peak in August 2004 and 3 million in 2012. The decrease is possibly due to the huge increase in number of projects in the last decade providing competition to the initial huge projects for participants. News stories about the project have appeared in almost all major media outlets including the *New York Times*, CNN, the Discovery Channel and National Public Radio. Ironically, the project was born due to the United States Congress's decision in 1993 to end SETI funding. After several years of planning the project leaders decided to launch the project that appealed to the general public's fascination with extra-terrestrial life and their desire to utilize an otherwise wasted resource as opposed to the grant-withholding bureaucrats and politicians.

Who does SETI? To answer that question, the team at SETI conducted a poll (Anderson, 2003) that showed that 92 per cent of SETI@home users are male, and that most of them are motivated primarily by their interest in the underlying science: they want to know if intelligent life exists outside earth.

Another major motivational factor is public acknowledgement. SETI@home keeps track of the contribution of each user (i.e. the amount of computation performed) and provides numerous web-site 'leader boards' where users are listed in order of their contribution. Users can also form 'teams', which have their own leader boards. The team mechanism turned out to be very effective for recruiting new participants.

As with GIMPS and other VDC projects, SETI@home participants have contributed more than CPU time. Volunteers have translated the SETI@home website into 30 languages, and have developed many kinds of add-on software and ancillary websites.

Various 'communities' have formed around SETI@home. There is a single worldwide community, which interacts through the SETI@home website. There are also national or language-specific communities, with their own websites and message boards. Some SETI@home user groups, such as the one in Germany hold annual conventions. Anderson claims that at least three couples have met and married through SETI@home communities.

But what is SETI? It stands for Search for Extra-Terrestrial Intelligence and it has been pursued with great interest by the US and Russia in particular in recent decades. The modern SETI era can be defined as beginning in 1959. In that year, Cornell physicists Giuseppe Cocconi and Philip Morrison published an article in *Nature* in which they pointed out the potential for using microwave radio to communicate between the stars.

A young radio astronomer, Frank Drake, had independently reached the same conclusion, and in the spring of 1960 conducted the first microwave radio search for signals from other solar systems. While he did not detect any signal of extraterrestrial origin, Drake's Project Ozma, spurred the interest of others in the astronomical community, most immediately the Russians.

In the 1960s, the Soviet Union dominated SETI, and it frequently adopted bold strategies. Rather than searching the vicinities of nearby stars, the Soviets used nearly-omnidirectional antennas to observe large chunks of sky, counting on the existence of at least a few very advanced civilizations capable of radiating enormous amounts of transmitter power.

At the beginning of the 1970s, NASA's Ames Research Centre in Mountain View, California began to consider the technology required for an effective search. A team of outside experts on leave from the Hewlett-Packard Corporation, produced a comprehensive study for NASA known as Project Cyclops. The Cyclops report provided an analysis of SETI science and technology issues that is the foundation upon which much subsequent work is based.

As the perception grew that SETI had a reasonable prospect for success, the Americans once again began to observe. During the 1970s, many radio astronomers conducted searches and by the late-1970s, SETI programs had been established at NASA's Ames Research Center and at the Jet Propulsion Laboratory (JPL) in Pasadena, California. These groups arrived at a dual-mode strategy for a large-scale SETI project. Ames would examine 1,000 Sun-like stars in a Targeted Search, capable of detecting weak or sporadic signals. JPL would systematically sweep all directions in a Sky Survey. In 1988, after a decade of study and preliminary design, NASA Headquarters formally adopted this strategy, and funded the program. Four years later, on the 500th anniversary of Columbus' arrival in the New World, the observations began. Within a year, Congress terminated funding.

With NASA no longer involved, both researchers and interested members of the public saw a diminished chance to answer, within their lifetimes, the profound question addressed by SETI. Then the possibility of pursuing SETI via Voluntary Distributed Computing emerged. Based at University of California, Berkeley, SETI@home is bringing millions of people from all over the world into this scientific quest. It has successfully harnessed competitive impulses for the good of science, offering insights into how to recruit and retain individuals in collective action on the Internet.

Einstein@home http://einstein.phys.uwm.edu

Einstein@home merits particular attention because of the understanding it yields of the variegated roles in VDC, in particular the role of the scientist who is embedded in traditional scientific institutions but who is also the critical bond between those institutions and the mass of volunteers on the project. Einstein@home uses VDC to search for gravitational waves or wrinkles in time, in the universe. It all began with Albert Einstein. Einstein revolutionized understanding of the universe and set the course for physics research in the twentieth century. Einstein posited that ripples exist in the fabric of time and space, that we live in a universe full of gravitational waves. He proposed that exploding stars, colliding black holes and other violent events create waves that alter space and time. Until now, these waves had not been detected because the task requires tools sensitive enough to measure very small effects. As Bruce Allen, the Principal Investigator and instigator of Einstein@home says: 'It's like trying to detect a change in the distance from the earth to the sun equal to the width of an atom'. Because of these challenges, concrete proof of Einstein's prediction has not yet been found.

Einstein@home, a relatively new VDC project (started in 2005) is an attempt to find that proof of those gravitational waves. Technology has caught up with Einstein's prediction and there now exist detectors sensitive enough to see these waves. Work Units received by users for Einstein@home consist of 12-megabyte data chunks from two of these detectors, the US Laser Interferometer Gravitational wave Observatory (LIGO) and the British-German GEO-600 gravitational wave observatory as they work together to find gravitational waves from stars and black holes. This data portrays only a very small fraction of the celestial sphere, thus allowing a user's computer to rigorously and thoroughly scour the data over several days in search of a gravitational wave. These experiments require enormous amounts of data to be processed, so the LIGO group created Einstein@home to use private computers to process LIGO and GEO 600 data.

What is the significance of this research? The discovery of gravitational waves would be monumental for both theoretical and experimental physics if found. Their existence would confirm much of Einstein's theory and provide us with a better understanding of the universe.

Led by Professor Bruce Allen, Einstein@home uses the BOINC infrastructure to host and distribute its data to volunteers. It is a notable project for the effort and attention put into the project home page by Professor Allen and his team of scientists and systems administrators. It has profiles and a picture of each volunteer, there is a Volunteer of the Day featured each day, and there are Certificates of Discovery awarded to individuals who make key discoveries. Although Einstein@ home consistently has a high level of volunteers from all over the world, this masks the fact that there is a huge turnover of volunteers with a small minority in for a long time. For Allen, this is the big challenge as he recognizes that a project is only as stable as its ability to recruit and retain volunteers.

3. Earth Science Projects

ClimatePrediction.Net http://www.climateprediction.net/

The multi-faceted nature of the most pressing challenges facing society today, and the necessary cooperative response to meeting those challenges, is exemplified in the issue of climate change. That, combined with the desire of many individuals to participate in working towards a solution, yet who are shut out of most of the key institutions which have the capacity to do something, lies behind the great interest in ClimatePrediction.net.

What does the future hold for the weather on Earth? ClimatePrediction.net is a VDC that is attempting to study the possibilities that are in store for Earth's climate in the next century. It aims to produce predictions of the Earth's climate up to 2100 and to test the accuracy of climate models. Climate prediction is an extremely computationally intense problem. Some of the fastest supercomputers in the 1980s and 1990s were doing meteorology. Then, a single computer sitting in a single place, usually costing tens of millions or hundreds of millions of dollars and owned by a single entity, was the only location for this type of research; today, equivalent computing power is harnessed by using thousands of PCs everywhere in the world for free. With VDC, running a model thousands of times with small variations allows scientists to study the sensitivity of the environment to changes in variables like carbon dioxide or the sulfur cycle. Participants are given their own climate model to run on their computer. With the screen saver that comes with the software, users can watch their own version of Earth as precipitation forms, temperatures change, pressure rises and falls, and many other characteristics evolve. At the completion of the run, results are returned to ClimatePrediction.net for analysis. So far, ClimatePrediction.net has allowed scientists to see that global warming may be more of a problem than previously believed. Simulations of ocean churning have provided more insight on the effects of thermohaline circulation as well.

ClimatePrediction.net made an impressive 3-D Open GL visualization package to show model output to the user. Climate change and weather are easy to appreciate and understand, and it is easy to visualize some scientific problems, i.e. compared to radio telescope (SETI@home) or LIGO (Einstein@home) data. The ClimatePrediction.net graphics show the user's currently running model and the user's 'world' full of clouds, snow and sea ice. Different views show temperature, precipitation and pressure. Thus, volunteers can follow their 'world' as it evolves through time. For more advanced users, they can get an add-on package that allows them to analyze the climate model data files on their computer. There is a separate graphics package developed independently by an enthusiastic participant of the project.

CPDN has been particularly good at, and fortunate in getting, a lot of publicity. The subject of two BBC documentaries and numerous news stories, each media 'spike' has drawn thousands of people into the project. The Project is notable for harnessing individual political concern and willingness to engage in global problem-solving.

Quake-Catcher. http://qcn.stanford.edu/

Individuals concerned with one natural phenomenon, earthquakes that wreak havoc on societies, particularly poor societies, can make use of the ubiquity of laptops and mobile phones. The Quake-Catcher Network (QCN) allows scientists to monitor earthquakes and quantify ground shaking with unprecedented spatial resolution through data gathered from citizen volunteers. The QCN, a collaborative research project between Dr Elizabeth Cochran of the US Geological Survey and Dr Jesse Lawrence of Stanford University, uses computers that are installed with software and special sensors to record moderate-to-large earthquakes and aftershocks. Citizen volunteers have the sensors installed externally to their desktop computers or internally to their laptop computers. These computers become seismic stations by providing the physical infrastructure, computer, internet connection, power, and the location and measurement of seismic activity. The computers are then networked using volunteer distributed computing techniques that allow scientists to monitor the sensors and retrieve earthquake data automatically.

The idea came from an everyday feature of technology. Every laptop has an accelerometer that is continually recording the acceleration of the laptop. It is not accelerating at all when sitting on a desk. If it is dropped to the ground, the accelerometer records a big acceleration and then a big deceleration when it hits the ground. The purpose of installing the accelerometer was to prevent owners claiming on warranty for damage sustained by dropping the laptop. Cell phones also have accelerometers. Cell phones are carried in pockets, in backpacks, but again, it is a question of data analysis, as earthquakes can be recorded when all cell phones in a region record the same type of movement at the same time.

Dr. Elizabeth Cochran, a geophysicist with the US Geological Survey came up with the ingenious idea of using a sensor installed in laptops to track earthquakes. She and her colleagues devised a project that can access accelerator data from thousands of participant laptops, so it can tell if all of them jump at the same time.

Who benefits? Everyone, but Southern California already has a network of earthquake detectors. Trying to get a network like that in somewhere like Indonesia is much harder so this project has great potential for addressing risks in poorer areas of the world that are prone to earthquakes. The value to science and society was recognized when, in 2012, Dr Cochran was named one of President Obama's recipients of the Presidential Early Career Awards for Scientists and Engineers, the highest honour bestowed by the United States government on science and engineering professionals in the early stages of their independent research careers. USGS Director Dr Marcia McNutt stated: 'As was clearly demonstrated by the recent Japanese experience, even a few seconds of warning before an earthquake can reduce the loss of life and property. Dr Cochran's innovative research will help make the nation safer from this natural hazard'.

'The Quake-Catcher Network is a way to involve the public in scientific data collection in high-risk earthquake and aftershock zones in the United States and around the world and to collect seismic data in non-traditional ways', said Cochran. Since then, volunteers have popped up in just about every state in the United States and across the world.

4. Biological Sciences Projects

Folding@home http://folding.stanford.edu

A project which links individual well-being to societal and community welfare and deployment of resources is Folding@home. Many of the individuals involved are motivated by the personal helplessness of watching loved ones die of diseases for which the cure is still being sought, and the political helplessness of seeing allocation of public money not being based of the alleviation of human suffering but political interests. We all have proteins in our bodies that are constantly folding and when they misfold they can result in misfolding related diseases like Alzheimer's, Parkinson's or Huntington's. Professor Vijay Pande of Stanford University's Departments of Chemistry and Structural Biology, leads the project that seeks to understand how the chains of amino acids that make up a protein are able to reliably and repeatedly fold into the shape required for proper function, the circumstances under which proteins fail to achieve the proper state, and the functional effects of that failure.

This investigation is performed using a molecular dynamics simulation that places each atom in an appropriate initial condition (position and velocity) given its expected position relative to other atoms and the temperature. The equations of motion for each particle are integrated as the system is evolved from the folded to the unfolded state. Thousands of simulations are run in parallel and are used as an ensemble comparison to dynamical experiments.

Accurate simulation of these biophysical processes requires vast computing resources. Folding@home is a distributed computing system first released in 2000 to provide such resources needed to simulate protein folding and other biomolecular phenomena. The way proteins fold has a significant impact on their function, as a protein's three dimensional shape has a massive impact on the role it plays in the human body. You can have the same constituent atoms or molecules but folded in a different way and it would follow that their function would be completely different. This is extremely important for finding cures for certain diseases, and explanations for certain deficiencies.

The Folding@home project has resulted in several papers being published in peer reviewed journals. It is basic science – it is not going to lead to a cure immediately – but it will lead to advances which might lead to cures five or ten years down the line. If this basic research is not done then the building blocks for an advanced cure will not be there.

For such a computationally heavy project, the cost of hiring a supercomputer was prohibitive. VDC computing power stepped into the breach and now boasts more power than can typically be gathered and operated locally due to the cost, physical space, and electrical/cooling load required for a supercomputer.

The user statistic website is in many ways the heart and soul of any volunteer distributed computing project, and Folding@home is no different. It allows volunteers to see how much they are contributing. The statistics server is a large database storing every result ever received by Folding@home and the credits (points) assigned to each user and team. Log files from all of the work servers are gathered up periodically and the completed work is credited to the volunteer and team for public display.

The forums, which are run by dedicated volunteers, offer users of Folding@home both technical support and a sense of community. They also get a great deal of helpful feedback on the forums that allows them to learn what features users want and what problems they are having. The website is the central location for all of the information on Folding@home, and includes news, answers to frequently asked questions, results, and papers. It also features a blog by Professor Pande, which communicatively connects the participants and the scientific team.

Folding@home, with support from Intel, Sony, ATI/AMD and NVIDIA, has been able to develop client applications that run on a wide variety of platforms including Microsoft Windows, Mac OS x Intel/PowerPC and Linux Intel. It has beta level support for NVIDIA and AMD GPUs. It is also available for the Sony PlayStation 3 video-game console, through Sony network distribution channels. And in fact, the majority of its performance is derived from GPU and PlayStation 3 platforms.

5. The Catch-all Classification of Everything Else

Motivations to engage in VDC projects are complex, social and sometimes defy conventional rationales or categorization. In the early days (early 1990s) this category was dominated by a project called DIMES which tried to map the Internet, trying to find out where every node is and what computers are connected to each other, through sending messages or ICMP (Internet Control Messaging Protocol). Today projects range from the frivolous to the World Community Grid, which studies a variety of problems in biology, medicine and the environment. There are a number of projects under this umbrella Grid, including the Clean Energy Project which tries to find the best organic compounds for solar cells and energy storage devices; and Computing for Clean Water, using the techniques of molecular dynamics to determine the fluid dynamics of water filters that are composed of nanotubes.

BOINC http://boinc.berkeley.edu

BOINC is an example of an institution that has emerged from a field of endeavour that is 'in flux' technologically and socially. Innovative, and meeting the requirements of the users who have built and maintain it, it demonstrates how human 'doing' and 'interaction' define problems and produce solutions to those problems as they arise. BOINC or the Berkeley Open Infrastructure for Network Computing, is arguably the home of VDC today and provides software for any scientist and scientific project and multiple projects for volunteers to choose from.

In the early days of VDC projects (1995–2003) it became apparent that there were technical and social challenges to running the projects and maintaining participation. Conducting a public computing project requires adapting an application program to various platforms, implementing server systems and databases, keeping track of user accounts and credit, dealing with redundancy and error conditions, and many other technical tasks. The principal technical challenge, once the initial project software was written and a server set up by the project, was making sure the software would run on the various platforms that the diverse body of participants or volunteers were using. Applications were needed for Windows Intel, Linux 86, Linux 86_4, Mac OS Power PCs, NVIDIA GPUS, among several others, and new variations were coming out all the time. Producing applications and fixing glitches in the software that showed up in particular platforms was a demanding and time consuming job. Most of the projects had one or two full-time system administrators employed, but it was difficult to keep up with the technical tasks. The social challenge was recruiting new participants and holding on to existing ones.

BOINC proved useful for helping with both of these challenges.

Funded by the National Science Foundation, BOINC is a multiproject/multiplatform volunteer computing infrastructure. It provides an infrastructure for hosting individual computationally heavy projects on their own servers, so that projects are independent from one another and do not share resources. The stability it offers, with much less problems for the volunteers on the user-end, leads to both a much higher completion rate of work and a higher retention rate. Carl Christensen, wrote about CPDN in 2005: 'About a third of users and machines [were] still active after 6 months. The original ClimatePrediction.net has a much higher attrition rate' (Christensen et al., 2005: 5). The reason was mainly technical, as CPDN's own platform was inadequate for the variety of configurations and machines out there. There were also less problems with the long-run work units sent out by CPDN and people stopped giving up so quickly.

BOINC was created at the University of California, Berkeley by the Space Sciences Laboratory, a group involved with the SETI@home project and is led by David Anderson. It is significant because it is the first computing tool that allows any scientist to use high-powered computing to run computationally expensive projects. BOINC makes it fairly easy and cheap to convert an existing application to a public computing project. BOINC projects are autonomous; each one maintains its own servers and databases, and does not depend on others. Some of these projects such as modelling Earth's future climate are so computationally intense that without this system, they would not even be attempted. Thus, research problems that were once considered impossible can now be investigated wherever there is a computer (Anderson, 2003; Christensen et al., 2005).

Although each project has its own server to host the program and data, there is a common graphical user-interface for those volunteers who download BOINC and they access individual projects through that interface. This programme named the BOINC manager presents a graphical interface with the BOINC client. The BOINC project makes versions of the BOINC client available for Microsoft windows, Apple Mac OS X, and Linux. The BOINC client is quite portable and can be compiled successfully on other operating systems (Korpela 2012). So, using a single instance (a single unique copy of an object) of the BOINC client, participants can register with multiple projects, and can control how their resources are shared (for example, a user might devote 60 per cent of her CPU time to studying global warming, and 40 per cent to SETI).

Because the users share the same interface, through which they access their own project(s), they are exposed to the large variety of other projects out there, and if for any reason they cannot or do not want to crunch data for their project of origin, they can select one or more of the other projects to join. As Christensen (2005) noted, once CPDN joined BOINC and there was a steady increase of BOINC users; this makes for a larger pool of active users than with the original ClimatePrediction.net project. It appears that as BOINC users on the projects that brought them into BOINC find a new project of interest to attach to, they tend to stay with the project unless repeated errors force them to give up on the project.

Projects that use the BOINC platform can effectively share the user base, and projects can co-exist in the BOINC client where the user has full control over what percentage of CPU time to give to a particular project. And even for users dedicated to one project, occasionally the project website will be down, or the project will be offline for maintenance, which could lead the user to try another project. The 'resource sharing' provided by BOINC seems to help projects such as ClimatePrediction.net, as users can see the longer-term benefits of contributing to many projects (and gain the credit for helping each project).

The users also stay because of the community aspect and the competition aspect as they compete to rack up credits for work units completed. The community aspect is often inextricably linked with the competitive aspect, as volunteers form communities and teams within that community in order to compete against teams from other communities. Each BOINC project is given a website template to create the communities; so one will find a home page, a message board, and a credit system that is the basis for user and team leader boards for any BOINC project.

On the message board, individuals are able to discuss whatever interests them, such as questions about the projects, the science behind the particular topic, or interesting results they have encountered.

The message boards encourage the formation of sub-communities, each of which in turn develops respective teams. Teams encourage the formation of individual relationships and make real-life gatherings a possibility. Because the projects have large numbers of participants (for example, SETI@home has about 135,000 active users), the community relies on the messages boards to break the group down by sub-interests; examples of sub-interests include common nationality or a common reason for joining the project. The sub-communities' significantly smaller size in turn makes individual relationships more of a reality. For example, language-specific communities as well as national communities have developed their own sites and message boards similar to that of the worldwide project page.

One interviewee described BOINC as a 'dating agency'. Paul, a GIMPS volunteer (which is a stand alone project not in BOINC) stated:

> Although BOINC itself may not set up these long lasting collaborations or in depth discussions what it does do is allow members of one community to explore other communities and then following exploration decide "hey I like these people, I will become an active member of that community"…it's a dating agency.

On BOINC, on the front page of each project, leader boards organized by individual, computer, and team are displayed prominently, illustrating the importance in the sub-community. The boards display the number of credits accrued by each individual, computer, and team. Every Work Unit processed accrues credits and the more credits accrued the greater is the contribution to the project. Individuals and teams engage in vigorous competition to accrue the most credits and a social prestige system emerges which rewards those who crunch the most data, and hence contribute the most to the project. A large number of credits elicits a correspondingly large number of responses to message board posts. The sub-communities beget real-life events in the same way that a school honour society or fraternity holds meetings and reunions, and release publications and newsletters.

For example, the German SETI@home community has held conventions for several years.

Indisputably, BOINC has facilitated a significant expansion of VDC Projects, as it provides a standard client, server, and statistics system, but with this fixed architecture comes limitations on the types of projects it can accommodate (Beberg, 2009). GIMPS for example prefers to maintain its own server and independence, not so much for technical reasons but for the fact that it is interested in a particular kind of volunteer, those interested in the substantive area of mathematics, and the volunteers in GIMPS and its founder, George Woltman, feel that BOINC is particularly amenable to recruiting people who are primarily motivated by the race for credits. Similar concerns by the CPDN community engendered a heated debate about whether to switch over to BOINC. That debate resulted in the transition which had tangible positive results, a more stable client and volunteers who stuck with the project. Whether they are the volunteers who are motivated by the science as much as, or instead of, the competition aspect is unclear. For most projects the advantages of BOINC greatly outweigh the disadvantages of not being in it.

In sum, the projects discussed and researched here exemplify sociologically significant aspects of VDC. GIMPS demonstrates the power of key individuals' actions and interaction in building a 'virtual' institution that engenders loyalty and longevity among volunteers. SETI@home shows the power of competition and game-playing to promote collaboration for altruistic goals. ClimatePrediction.net (CPDN) witnesses the emergence of a new means for individuals to engage in or contribute to pressing but difficult to address global challenges, such as in this case, climate change. Einstein@home shows how key individuals are particularly important in navigating the intersection of traditional institutions, in this case, universities, and emerging ones that are based on 'networked individuals' (Rainie and Wellman, 2012). Finally, BOINC demonstrates how institutional innovation is particularly possible and significant in a time of technological flux. Together, the social processes offer a window into changes that are not just affecting science, but also business, the arts, and civic society, all the fields where individuals and institutions can work together to achieve set goals.

Chapter 3

Breaking Down the Walls: Voluntary Distributed Computing and Citizen Science

Voluntary Distributed Computing emerged after a time when science's relationship with the public was at a low ebb. In the mid-1990s, Carl Sagan observed that the general public's attitude toward science was increasingly one of alienation and even hostility. Two questions arise: if this is true, why had such alienation and hostility arisen? Secondly, given the alacrity and loyalty with which VDC participants participate, and the success of other 'citizen science' endeavours (Nielsen, 2011), is there evidence that there is a new engagement in and enthusiasm for science emerging because of a new ability to participate? It is certainly made possible by the changes enabled by new information and communication technologies: the overcoming of physical and cost barriers to participation in the production and communication of knowledge, and the rise of 'empowered or networked individuals' who can connect and collaborate with each other. But such individuals and collaborative endeavours must also connect and collaborate with the existing structures and institutions of science, which are primarily hierarchical. The tremendous growth of these institutions in the twentieth century facilitated scientific advances but also kept science behind the walls of those same science establishments and institutions.

Under industrial capitalism, science went increasingly behind the physical walls of universities and institutes and behind the prestige walls of professionalization and accreditation. Research took place in university research departments or private Research and Development labs, usually affiliated to pharmaceutical companies. Professionals and academics were accredited by universities, were members of professional and academic organizations, and published their findings in costly peer reviewed journals. This structuring was a necessary step in building a modern society. Although Weber (1947) feared the 'iron cage of rationality' – being caught up in the rules and regulations of hierarchical organizations to the exclusion of the human and creative element – he also recognized that large hierarchies were a necessary step or component in building the institutions required in a modern society. The critical point is that the technologies of the time determined the organizational structures and institutional practices. Today with the Information and Communication Technology revolution (Castells, 1996; 2000), technologies are enabling different types of structures and practices. Prior to the advent of the distributed science allowed by the BOINC architecture, a large computationally heavy science project's accessibility would be limited to a select number of researchers, most likely from established universities. External access was limited as were outside opinions and ideas. By placing the discussion and projects in the public domain, VDC, especially as enabled by BOINC, promises to overcome this limitation. Thus, research communities that include lay volunteers on a larger, global scale have the impressive power to shape the course of a project. Although most VDC projects are part of academic institutions and established science centres, GIMPS has shown that research projects and discoveries can be done outside established institutions of academia also, and be accepted by the scientific community at large.

However, VDC is still in its infancy and the democratization of science enabled by the fewer barriers to knowledge production that the Internet offers has not yet crystallized into institutional paths. Just as in the economic sphere, the physical and cost barriers for the production of information have come down. Just as there is a transformation in the production and dissemination of news, so in the scientific field the tumbling of physical and cost barriers is beginning to be felt. VDC is timely, not just in using hitherto unused resources and allowing non-professionals to participate, but also because time on supercomputers is expensive and scientific research is increasingly reliant on heavy computation. VDC software allows researchers access to supercomputing power for research that is computationally intense at a much lower cost with the help of volunteers' computers around the globe. BOINC, the platform for the majority of VDCs is funded by public money and this has already yielded significant measurable returns (and the less tangible benefits of participation in and opening up of science to citizens) and has enormous potential returns as the fraction of computers participating is a tiny percentage of the total number in the world.

Science as an Institution

Science is not, as some scientists would argue, a uniquely rational enterprise that is, or should be, radically independent from everything else, but is an institution whose existence is interwoven with a network of other institutions which gave it life and continue to sustain it. And, as Weber observed, once science becomes part of this network of institutions, it begins to affect them, and vice versa.

But what is an 'institution'? Most simply, an institution is the rules and shared meanings that define social relationships, help define who occupies what position in these relationships, and guide interaction by giving actors cognitive frames or sets of meanings to interpret the behaviour of others.

Or, as Nielsen (2011) describes, they are what happens when people are inspired by a common idea, so inspired that they coordinate their actions in pursuit of that idea (Nielsen, ibid., 169). The actors here are both professional scientists and the different professional positions within scientific organizations, the organizations themselves, including universities, private laboratories, and government research institutes, and their practices: the conduct of research and the sharing at conferences with each other and the publication of their findings in peer-reviewed journals.

Action in institutions is constrained not only by structural position but also by the organization's cognitive and normative orientation (Meyer, Scott and Deal, 1981; Powell and DiMaggio, 1983). New institutionalist theories concern how fields of action[1] come into existence, remain stable and can be transformed. While an organizational practice may have its origins in certain rational principles, it can become institutionalized over time and continue to be used even though it may no longer be beneficial to the organization (Zucker, 1977; 1987; 1989; Roy, 1997; Fligstein, 1985; 1990).[2] Scientific practices during the twentieth century became institutionalized and are resistant to change, even regarding those aspects which are no longer beneficial to the research institution itself or to science. Scientific organizations are now in an environment where communication technologies and the behavioural changes that go with them are breaking down the physical and technological barriers surrounding participation in science and are opening up the questions: who can be a scientist? What does it mean to be a scientist? How is the practice of science changing? What does this mean for the relationship between science and society? Can VDC contribute to a new public engagement in science? Are the old 'establishment' walls becoming more porous?

In turbulent times or environments, rules can be made from laws in intended or unintended ways and/or can be borrowed from other fields to create new institutions. Individuals with appropriate social skills can create new social orders or 'fields' through their ability to get others to cooperate with them (Fligstein, 2001; McAdam and Fligstein, 2012). Key individuals in VDC are doing precisely this. Technology developments are usually the main driver of institutional innovation, and the Internet is making it much easier to create institutions, by spreading ideas and helping coordinate action. Historically, big changes in the role of science have often been driven by new technologies and the new institutions they enable. The printing press had a critical role as enabler of the Renaissance, the Reformation and the Enlightenment. Most of the time institutions change slowly. But today is not most of the time. Linux, Wikipedia and now VDC demonstrate how, with the Internet and the social changes it brings about, it has become much easier to create new institutions and transform or reinvent existing ones.

---

1   'Fields' or 'arenas' or 'games' are local social orders. Fields (Bourdieu 1977, Bourdieu and Wacquant, 1992) refer to situations where organized groups of actors gather and frame their actions vis-à-vis one another.

2   The institutional claim that social and cultural pressures lead to organized conformity builds on philosophical underpinnings of German idealists and phenomenologists most clearly represented in the writings of Berger and Luckmann (1967). Social reality is a human construct and a by-product of repetitive interactions. Thus organizational activities become institutionalized, taking the form of 'rationalized myths' when repeated over a period of time (Meyer and Rowan, 1977). The idea that the formal structure may be embraced as myth and ceremony in order to signal legitimacy lies at the very heart of the new institutional perspective. Indeed, once a threshold of firms adopt an innovation, most future adoption, especially in an uncertain environment, is more likely to result from mimetic, coercive or normative isomorphism than from competition (DiMaggio and Powell, 1981).

Ordinary people are participating in scientific research in ways unimaginable a generation ago. Although it is not going to become the primary means of doing scientific research, VDC has a potential role that will make it very much a part of the global 'institution' of scientific research.

Breaking Down the Walls: The Sharing of Scientific Research Findings

Science, over the last two hundred years, has increasingly gone behind 'walls'. This is evident in the output of science, most of which is published in journals which cost an enormous amount to access; most who access them are member of a university or research institute which has a group subscription to thousands of journals. As much of basic science in particular is funded with public money, this practice is coming under increasing criticism from the public and from concerned scientists 'inside' the walls, articulated through the 'Open Access' movement, which advocates the practice of providing unrestricted access via the Internet to peer-reviewed scholarly journal articles.

Governments have responded with the Public Library of Science (PLoS), where scientists pay to have their journals published and it is then made freely available on the web. In the United States in 2008, the National Institutes for Health (NIH) public access policy requires anyone funded by the NIH to upload finished papers to an openly accessible archive within 12 months of publication in a conventional journal.

The Internet also allows empowered individuals, departments, and disciplines, to lead the way. Physics has done so with the preprint arXiv. A 'preprint' is a scientific paper, often at late draft stage, ready to be considered by a scientific journal for publication, but not yet published in a journal. Most physicists put up preprints, all available for free download. It has revolutionized physics by speeding up the rate at which scientific discoveries can be shared. Also, it has made much of humanity's knowledge about physics freely accessible to anyone with an internet connection.

The most obvious benefit is to individual citizens who can now access scientific knowledge, but there is also huge benefit for poorer societies, whose universities cannot afford to subscribe to the journals and whose ability to foster indigenous innovation is dependent on being able to access research findings by their peers around the globe. Society's best interests have shifted away from the old business model. The technologies have changed, but not the business model.

Some of the most prominent scientists 'behind the walls' are now able – and do – engage with interested members of the public, and also indeed scientists from other institutions, via blogs and the conversations that ensue. Several scientists who use VDC as part of their research strategy do this successfully, and it is a critical component in retaining volunteers, as proactive and accessible Principal Investigators (PIs) invariably have high performing VDC projects. Projects that fade away quickly or stay lacklustre in terms of recruiting and retaining participants almost never have a PI that is visible and accessible. As Neilsen (ibid.) observed, blogs make it possible for anyone with an Internet connection to get an informal, rapid fire glimpse into the minds of many of the world's greatest scientists. It is not just the scientific content that matters, it is the culture that is revealed, a particular way of viewing the world.

Vijay Pande, the lead scientist on the Stanford University based Folding@ home project writes a blog on the Folding@home website that gives insight into the science and the practice and culture shaping the research. Bruce Allen, the lead scientist on Einstein@home is a visible and accessible presence on the project website. He responds and answers queries personally on a daily basis for Einstein@home. He argues that it is a part of his daily routine as much as engaging with his colleagues inside the physical and virtual walls of his university research base and professional sphere.

Breaking Down the Walls: The Changing Requirements of Scientific Research

Computation is now an essential element of almost all scientific research. Even if VDC projects do not get additional funding, having access to computational ability that they wouldn't otherwise have access to means that they can do research without the level of funding that they would otherwise require for access to supercomputing facilities. Computation is central to all scientific research now and a lot of scientists are not necessarily computer savvy. Chris Walsall, a volunteer on the GIMPS project, described how the norm is increasingly that 'you need a programming, geek kind of person partnered with the scientist to determine what is it they want calculated, how they want to calculate it'.

There is a need for those with those skills and interest to be 'pulled' into scientific endeavours. One such person, Paul, a long time participant in VDC, has an eclectic history of scientific activity. He says:

> I'm really a computer person. My degree is chemistry and I have a D Phil in physical chemistry. I discovered computers while I was a student. Although I was always interested in mathematics, I'm not really a professional mathematician in any sense. I've been playing with computers my entire professional life. I've always considered myself a scientist of one kind or another. I'm a generalist rather than a specialist so my professional career is a wide variety of activities. I've started out life as chemist, I've since been a nuclear physicist, a roboticist, I've done computer security, kyrpto, infomatics.

However, there are some computational problems that do not map well to VDC because they require very large datasets to be maintained in close proximity. Even then though a significant portion of the work can be done by VDC. Chris Walsall recalls:

A fellow by the name of Fred factored P to the power of 21-1, it required access to a supercomputing grid with a massive amount of memory to be able to do the final matrix analysis. This is the kind of thing where the initial relations work is able to be calculated by VDC but the final steps had to be done on a large computer, multi-core, with a large amount of memory. VDC is not a panacea, there are some solutions that map well to it, and there are some problems that simply do not.

Over the last two centuries, the only feasible way to tackle complex problems was through a hierarchical organization; to pay all those people to come together and form a hierarchy organized into managers and subordinates. But without money it has historically been difficult to hold such complex creative projects together.

George Woltman, the founder of GIMPS argues that VDC enables a different way of tackling complex problems:

> I think there's a lot of potential. If you don't get a large government grant to buy supercomputer time to test out your theory, more people with more theories can go out and get the computing power to test their theories, and hopefully someone will have a correct theory and solve one of our problems. It increases our chances of solving major problems.

This is what the author Clay Shirkey has described as the potential unleashed when you match technological developments with potential universal access: 'Now we can do big things for love' (2010: 154). He considers the number of hours spent watching TV and coined the phrase 'cognitive surplus' to describe our society's disposable time and energy – the time we collectively have when we are not dealing with the basic obligations of life, such as making a living and feeding our family. It is the time we put into leisure activities such as watching television, or going out with friends, or relaxing with a hobby. Mostly, these are activities we do alone or in small groups, and large groups are usually doing a simple activity like watching a soccer game. What online tools do is make it easy to coordinate complex creative projects in a large group, such as Voluntary Distributed Computing.

Bruce Allen, the Principal Investigator on Einstein@home, grasps the significance of this 'cognitive surplus' or what he calls 'distributed thinking'. He likens the situation to the phrase used by the Open-Source Movement: 'every bug is shallow [trivial] to someone', i.e. the more minds you have addressing a problem, the more likely solutions are going to emerge quickly and be robust solutions. It is not just in coming up with creative solutions to problems, it is the level of accuracy in detail which emerges from many minds addressing a fine-grained problem.

Allen says: 'I've come to respect our volunteers, I've seen some amazing things over the years. For instance, our work units have completely obscure names, like G_106.257_Ra...basically a string of numbers and letters and signs that goes on for 30 characters. Occasionally you'd get a message on the boards saying "I thought I was never supposed to get the same work twice. Six weeks ago I got the same G_106 etc...string of numbers and letters and signs that goes on for 30 characters. And I got it again yesterday". I thought "this can't happen, the system is designed so this can't happen". But I look anyway and you know, they were right. Somehow their mind can recognize this bunch of characters that turns up 6 weeks later'.

Problems Behind the Walls and Outside are Not So Different: Cheating

Fear of malfeasance or fraud has been one of the main arguements for scientists reluctant to use VDC. Occasionally people will try to cheat the system either because of malice and/or to get their rankings (in the competitive tables of data crunched by individuals or teams) bumped up. This has been recognized and dealt with in VDC through two strategies: double or triple crunching of each work unit to detect anomalies and outlier analysis, i.e. if results from one computer are way out of the results domain of a larger sample set, the alarm is raised and the problem is investigated. Scientists involved in VDC point out that malfeasance is also a problem that traditional institutions have to deal with. In fact, traditional institutions which have seen themselves and been seen as, the guardians of the 'rational' process, have been faced with the reality that scientific behaviour is embedded in an institutional context that shapes the purportedly 'rational' process.

Traditional institutions have not prevented scientific cheating and fraudulent behaviour. Fabrication of results is a serious problem; findings from a survey by the *British Medical Journal* published in 2012 found that 13 per cent of 2,700 UK-based scientists and doctors surveyed had witnessed colleagues fabricating or altering research data ahead of publication in peer-reviewed journals and 6 per cent admitted doing it themselves. And the problem is universal. Ince's (2011) account of cancer research at Duke University in the US showed a research project that was riddled with errors which the checks and balances supposedly built into journals, universities and individual professional integrity did not prevent.

A proper understanding of misbehaviour requires that attention be given to the negative aspects of the research environment. The modern scientist faces intense competition, and is further burdened by difficult, sometimes unreasonable, regulatory, social, and managerial demands. This mix of pressures creates many possibilities for the compromise of scientific integrity (Martinson et al., 2005). The chance of winning a prize – an independent academic position, tenure, scientific renown – motivates bioscience researchers but for most there is long hours, low pay and career uncertainty (Freeman et al. 2001).

Ince (ibid.) in his account of the Duke University cancer research scandal identified a major lesson for scientists as the need to recognize the now central role of computation in scientific research and to ensure adequate involvement and support of Information Technology professionals and statisticians. The emergence of new technologies is profoundly challenging the practice of science from biology to physics to zoology.

David Anderson of BOINC equated this need for technological expertise in what is now routine computationally heavy research with what VDC has to offer. The various skills and expertise needed for research now include computational resources. Anderson explains: 'Any one scientist or scientific project or department even if they are willing to use VDC does not have access to the combination of skills...the best way is for every research university to have a department which provides these for any scientist on campus. This also provides a way to ensure young, underfunded researchers can accelerate their research', thus addressing the broader negative aspects of the contemporary research environment for young scientists.

The prize of social prestige motivates the competitive crunchers in VDC and similarly such competition can produce malfeasance. The answer in both is institutional and policy related – for bioscientists to make careers more economically rewarding and productive, and for VDC scientists, to provide ways for contributors to feel unique, valued and recognized.

Accountability: Funding Science from Public Money

Much of basic science is funded by public money and is therefore legitimately eligible for scrutiny. Research funding is a term generally covering any funding for scientific research in the areas of both 'hard' science and technology and social science. Most research funding comes from two major sources, corporations (through research and development departments) and government (primarily carried out through universities and specialized government agencies). In the OECD, around two-thirds of research and development in scientific and technical fields is carried out by industry, and 20 per cent and 10 per cent by universities and government respectively, although in poorer countries the industry contribution is significantly less.

However, with some exceptions (e.g. biotechnology) government provides the bulk of the funds for *basic* scientific research. In commercial research and development, all but the most research-oriented corporations focus more heavily on near-term commercialization possibilities rather than 'blue-sky' ideas or technologies. Funding of research by private companies is mainly motivated by profit, and they are much less likely than governments to fund research projects solely for the sake of knowledge. The profit incentive causes researchers to concentrate their energies on projects which are perceived as likely to generate profits. Government-funded research can either be carried out by the government itself, or through grants to academics and other researchers outside the government. Often research funding is applied for by scientists and approved by a granting agency to financially support research. Total government research funding in most developed countries is between 1.5 per cent and 3 per cent of GDP (OECD, 2013).

Funding is scarce but VDC provides a big return in terms of the amount of work done for the money it is given. BOINC is funded by public money – grants from the National Science Foundation (NSF) in the United States. This allows it to employ four people and pay for hardware. But this level of investment is minimal compared to what is required for supercomputers or clusters of powerful computers and yet it can do an equivalent amount of computation. Several high profile VDC projects have experienced difficulty in getting funded and BOINC, based at the University of California, Berkeley, which has a record of excellence in research and is very competitive in getting NSF grants, has still felt like, to quote David Anderson 'a poor relation' in the family of scientists competing for grants.

Bruce Allen, the principal scientist of Einstein@home, says the situation is improving as VDC persists with minimal funding and shows results. When setting up Einstein@home, he applied for approximately two million dollars but the proposal was rejected. However, once the project was successfully launched, and got a lot of publicity,

> We put together another application and got 998,000 thousand dollars worth of funding which was supposed to last for two years but actually lasted for four.

The project recently got another round of funding from the NSF and they get support where they are based in Germany, keeping the project going. To put the high return on investment in context, Allen explains:

> The hardware we use is worth under 100,000 dollars and we use all open-source software [which is free]. The project is equivalent to 40,000 computers running 24 hours a day 7 days a week. If you wanted to set up a building with 40,000 computers in it, with electricity, cooling system, administrators to look after it, it would cost a lot of money. Just the electricity alone would be 8 million dollars per year. The hardware that we have in comparison to that is really quite small.

The funding of science by government, in particular basic science, is a public matter (Levine, 2007) and VDC can strengthen citizens' role in the policy process that decides funding priorities and focus. There is a political dimension to all VDC activity even if the participants are not reflexively political.

First and most directly, the distribution of goods by the state, the funding of science, is affected by VDC. The projects with the largest following can legitimately claim public support for research into their particular area and apply for government funding partially on the basis of this. VDC offers a direct and democratic mechanism for deciding research policy. Anderson (2003) points out that because computer owners can contribute to whatever project they choose, potentially the control over resource allocation for science will be shifted away from government funding agencies (with the myriad factors that control their policies) and towards the public.

Secondly, VDC projects call attention to particular areas, such as the funding of research into preventing malaria, that are neglected by public and private funders of medical research, primarily because the disease does not affect those in the countries where such funders are based. Malaria kills millions every year, yet is given the same amount of attention by public and private pharmaceutical research as acne medication. The VDC project Malaria.net allows members of the public who see this as politically unacceptable but are powerless to express it to not only make a political statement, but also to actively contribute to research in this area by signing up to the project. The audience or constituency for these projects is a global one but their existence provides points of leverage for domestically based advocacy groups (Keck and Sikkink, 1996). Individual citizens who care where their taxes are being spent and see many of the most critical problems facing themselves and their children as global problems can, through their participation in key VDC projects, put pressure on domestic governments but in an international interconnected framework.

A common theme among volunteers in almost all the projects I investigated was that there is an explicit political dimension in their involvement in VDC and in their choice of project. CPDN (ClimatePrediction.net) has an explicitly political goal – of raising awareness of climate change. Chris Walsall of GIMPS initially got involved in Distributed.net and says he was politically motivated to prove empirically as part of that project that the US government policy on legal encryption levels were inadequate at the time. Several respondents from Folding@ home cited inadequate or politically determined funding for particular diseases as motivating factors for involvement in that VDC project.

The Empowered Individual

Seeing VDC not only as a means to meet the computational requirements of a lot of scientific research, but also as a way to overcome the cost and institutional barriers of participation indicates the opportunities for 'the empowered individual' in science, both inside and outside established institutions. This raises the question of 'who is a scientist in today's world?'

Outside the scientific organizations, the idea of the empowered individual in science has an ancestor in the tradition of the amateur scientist. The grand tradition of amateurs making valuable contributions to the great discoveries of science is well-known. Even today, many fields, including astronomy, botany, and geology, continue to rely on the contributions of amateur collectors and observers to advance the state of the science outside the sphere of VDC. This makes amateur scientists an important addition to the institution of science.

Despite the difficulty amateurs have in discovering new scientific truths, and their even greater problems getting them published, the canon of scientific knowledge has been greatly expanded by people without an advanced scientific education. Many of the greatest scientific discoveries were made by amateurs with a passionate personal interest in their subject. George Mendel is famous for discovering the laws of inheritance and helping found the discipline of genetics. He had a bit of scientific training, mostly in physics, but spent most of his life in a Czech abbey as an Augustinian priest. It was here that he conducted his famous experiments with pea plants and discovered the dominant and recessive qualities of genes. Though the work laid the foundations for the science of genetics, his original paper on the subject was almost universally ignored.

The twentieth century was a time when increasingly, in the words of George Woltman, the founder of GIMPS, 'one could not make a contribution to scientific research without having a PhD in something'. Many talented and motivated people did not have the opportunity to pursue the traditional path into universities and research laboratories and under the conditions of industrial capitalism were permanently shut out of the field of science.

VDC addresses this in two ways. Most broadly, it allows many more people than traditional science to participate in any way in scientific research. Secondly, it allows people to actually make discoveries that advance human knowledge and are written into history books.

At the first level, millions of people have arguably stormed the barricades of science as an institution by becoming participants in the scientific process. The Internet, new technologies, and now VDC offer the opportunity for people to, at the most basic level, contribute to scientific research, even when their professional path did not follow the smooth and straight trajectory that traditional scientific careers require, with its limited professional positions. People who did not have the opportunity at a key time in their youth to pursue scientific training can now engage in the world of scientific research.

Lumley, a volunteer in GIMPS stated:

> Many people have had high aspirations when they were young. Just how many wanted to be a fireman or a ballerina but never did can never be known. My own ambition was to go into astrophysics. Along the way I discovered that although my algebra was top notch I just could not wrap my head well enough around calculus. That failure is a regret that I have, and though the search for prime numbers does not entail the direct use of calculus nor does it solve the meaning of the universe, the chance to work on a problem of purely mathematical abstraction without the need to train oneself for years is appealing to me.

A respondent in the 2010–11 online survey replied:

> I'm a college drop out. I have a bottom-tier IT job, and my ability to actually contribute to things that I care about in work is very limited. Fixing a printer jam just doesn't matter, but for a variety of reasons, that's the sort of work I've been stuck with, and will be stuck with for a very long time. However, I'm an intelligent autodidact, and was raised by a loving family. My current life makes

me feel like I'm letting them down, but working on DC projects, particularly ones that counter diseases that have affected our immediate family, gives me a sense that my life has been less of a waste.

Participants in VDC do make discoveries, though like traditional science in universities and research institutes, they are usually the outcome of long and painstaking involvement. When it happens, the personal satisfaction and reward, and the benefit to human knowledge, is the same. Mike Vang, the founder of the Mersenne Forum for the GIMPS project, did not finish high school but after years of learning and involvement in GIMPS, he made an original discovery and his name is now in a textbook that is used in mathematics classes in high schools across the US. He explains:

> On 27th of March 2010 I had 2 little computers running in the background, I checked them once a month and I opened up the window one day and I was like wow, the computer says it had found a factor. Now a few years ago, that happened to me and I had gotten all excited and when I went to tell somebody, they said if you look at it you can see it had already been found. So this time when I looked at the screen I thought it was just a mistake in the software (laughs), I told you I'm not a mathematician right. I had to go look to figure out what that number was. And I found out the last factor that had been found was in 1989. So that number was significant...it ended up being put into a book, a real text book. Some college or high school student is reading some boring text book in secondary school and then they'll see at the bottom a footnote on me, they'll glance at it and it won't mean anything. But for the rest of my life my name will be on that textbook.

Lumley, a volunteer for GIMPS, puts it this way:

> Probably the most compelling reason to run GIMPS is to get your name in the history books. Think of it. Mersenne himself lived and died hundreds of years ago and yet today his name is plastered all over an electronic medium of which he could never ever have conceived. All the discoverers of Mersenne primes have their names permanently etched in "stone", and although no one will remember most of their names from memory, they will still be there in the list, flagstones on the never ending path of mathematical discovery. Thousands of years from now their names will still be recorded somewhere as discoverers of Mersenne primes. This is no exaggeration either. As long as modern technology survives, so will their names.

Carl Sagan's lament at the level of alienation from science receives an antidote in the form of the responses from volunteers on what being able to engage in science through VDC means to them.

Table 3.1   Decision to Volunteers: Responses from 2010–11 survey of volunteers in VDC to question on role of science in their decision to give time and resources to VDC projects

DC has been a scientific leveller – you don't need to be a researcher at a rich university with a fast supercomputer now, a webserver at BOINC will suffice.

It allows me to contribute to science when I would be otherwise unable to do so.

I think that DC is a terrific accomplishment, both in terms of computational theory and practical application. It has made it possible to tackle challenges which would have been unthinkable without. It allows me to further scientific knowledge with almost no input required on my behalf. I would feel irresponsible if I did not participate.

It is a way for an individual to contribute, to a greater or lesser extent, in 'big science' or 'big math' – at least if you choose carefully.

It's a way for me to contribute to scientific advances. I'm in the social sciences and still consider myself somewhat of an idealist when it comes to the scientific community. If there's a reasonable way for me to help other researchers, I'm always happy to do so.

It's a way for me to contribute to cutting edge research without having to get a PhD in a field I don't actually want to pursue for the rest of my life. I also now dislike the notion of how much computing power is wasted or left idle so I feel like my computers are doing more for society than others.

I joined GIMPS because it is a way of contributing to pure mathematics research when I am unable to do so in other ways. I studies mathematics to bachelor level 25 years ago but did not take it further: so the interest is there and the desire to contribute too, but the technical ability is not. In this way, I can be part of modern research despite my grossly inadequate training.

It allows lay people to contribute something other than money to research.

It allows smaller groups to perform research on a scale they would otherwise be unable to afford. At the same time research that otherwise would not be done due to its low odds of being immediately profitable will still get done. [It is] laying a base for important scientific discoveries.

I think people benefit from being part of a research project. It makes science more tangible and hopefully promotes overall support for it.

While not all projects have meaningful or realistic scientific objectives, it is very important for scientists around the world to know that they can advance their field/ project even if they are on a limited budget/resources by harnessing the computer power of thousands of volunteers around the world.

DC is important to society because it provides massive computational resources to science AND it promotes a better relationship between science and the average joe.

Beyond the Walls: Public Education in Science

No research has been done on the impact of VDC on education but clearly participation provides opportunities for learning. Many of the participants learn a significant amount of science through participation and all improve their knowledge of technology. The potential for public education in the broad sense – on the scientific challenges of our age and our attempts to meet them – and in the narrower sense of individuals improving their knowledge and skills on specific issues is enormous. Not all VDC projects attempt to 'educate the public', but in practice that is what happens. Some have public education as an explicit part of their purpose, such as ClimatePrediction.net, which has been very successful in raising awareness of the issue of climate change, both in the home base of the project, the UK, and beyond. The use of the UM model (from UK MetOffice 'Unified Model') gives the public the opportunity to run a 'state of the art' climate model, and introduce them to such issues as global warming, climate research and climate modelling (Christensen et al., 2005).

The message boards on the project website encourage the formation of sub-communities, each of which in turn develops respective teams. Teams encourage the formation of individual relationships and discuss the project and the science behind it. For example, the ClimatePredicton.net forums commonly discuss the results of a world simulation. Perhaps the polar ice caps melted because the average world temperature jumped 12 degrees by the year 2065, or perhaps a scenario with double the CO_2 content resulted in nearly no effect on the earth's temperature. Users learn about climate science together, and put their new knowledge to use by discussing and interpreting the results of their models.

Chris Walsall, an experienced volunteer with GIMPS observed:

> With education [on the project] you can get somebody advancing to the point where they can actually contribute to the science themselves. It also comes back to the community aspect and colleagues...an example, a fellow who goes by the handle x..his real name is Bill..a young man starting university, doing a course in computer programming and he came on wanting to know which he should do, C or C++. A lot of the more seasoned programmers came in and gave him advice, and then he started posting some software he wrote, he was basically getting it peer reviewed. I've been programming for 25 years and there are more seasoned people than me, so he has some very high level people who can mentor/guide him. He's got to the point where he's taken on maintenance responsibility for one of the clients, the Lucas code.

However, the Internet also introduced some new barriers of its own, specifically the issue of access to the hardware and software, and the degree of literacy necessary to engage with it (DiMaggio et al., 2001). Klein (1999) identified factors that are still pertinent: the need for resources to invest in computer and communication hardware, monthly service fees, and computer skills, specifically effective expression in a text-based medium that requires a high level of education. These barriers make it likely that, at least in the near future, the Internet's democratic potential will be exploited by relatively elite groups of citizens with the money, access to technology, skills, and general education to use them.

Still, as more and more citizens gain access to the technology and as new generations of computer-literate school children mature into adult citizens, participation in online forums may become more broad-based. Certainly in VDC, once access is gained, the strength is that engagement is possible with people with very different levels of education, and a great deal of self-learning and mentorship goes on. Mike Vang of GIMPS recalls that

> I had to do hours and hours of work, and I'm being serious. I was smart but had no appropriate training, no mathematical training what so ever, no computer training so for me to do stuff its very, very difficult. Well, say for Garo [a participant in forum with a PhD in computer science] for example he'll do stuff and post about it in the forum and explain something and I'm like "wow" and then I do it and it works you know. If you ran through the programme and you could see how slowly I do everything. But the challenge was "can I really do this?" And I can. It's a lot of work; if I take the whole time that I've been alive, working with computers is the biggest thing that's happened to me.

A large number of highly educated people, such as Garo in Vang's quotation, are willing and happy to impart their knowledge and to do so through collaboration. This makes VDC a natural way of motivating and inspiring young people to participate in scientific research. The willingness and interest produces a type of mentoring system for neophytes and young people, the potential of which is very significant. VDC offers opportunities for scientific learning but also for civic education. Learning science and technology leads to interaction with other people, communities in forums, and the learners can see that they benefited from a community of people and often in turn contribute their own time and effort to that community or to newer learners coming onto the projects.

As volunteers gain knowledge and experience, the opportunities to learn continue to grow along with the projects, and many are inspired to work directly with the software to improve it. On the ClimatePrediction.net project for instance, where graphics are used to visualize data analysis, more advanced users can get an add-on package that allows them to analyze the climate model data files on their computer. There is even a separate graphics package developed independently by an enthusiastic participant of the project.

Lumley, a volunteer in VDC wrote:

> Being the first to put a man on the moon had great political value for the USA, but what was perhaps of the most lasting value to the society was the by-products of the race. By-products such as the new technologies and materials that were developed for the race, are now common everyday items.

Chris Walsall noted that the infrastructure developed for VDC and accompanying innovations can be used elsewhere. And of course BOINC was developed by the same team who set up SETI@home and has provided the tools for anyone with a project idea to start a VDC project.

Part of scientific research is testing findings or products under different conditions. VDC projects such as GIMPS provide a way for testing hardware and software, as there is a high-level team of testers available throughout the VDC community. Innovaters such as Chris Walsall find the VDC community is the perfect research community where others test his code, give feedback and generally improve it. Chris said:

> I love software and I'm a big fan of what I call "driving problems" where you have a problem, you go out, you write the software, you find a solution, and then make it available to the public. Also because the users of primenet and now GPU72 tend to be fairly sophisticated users, I find it is an excellent testbed for me to experiment with different technologies and get feedback from sophisticated users. And then apply the software to other projects where the users are not nearly so sophisticated.

Although many in GIMPS stress that the project is about building abstract knowledge and it does not have a practical application, in fact they are incorrect on two levels. Knowledge about Prime Numbers contributes to cryptography and hence internet security. Hardware can be tested using VDC programmes: software routines from the GIMPS project were used by Intel to test Pentium II and Pentium Pro chips before they were shipped. More prosaically, the technology and code developed for the project when applied to other projects, commercial projects outside VDC, save time by having been tested and any glitches ironed out through the VDC project. Chris Walsall explains:

> Outside DC, I do quite a bit of data driven websites for projects for different companies. Right now I'm working on a large project for an NGO here in Barbados. I can apply a lot of the technology I developed for GPU72 to that project and know that a lot of glitches are not going to show up and have unsophisticated users not know what is happening.

Prime programmes are particularly useful for testing hardware as they are intensely CPU and bus bound. They are relatively short, give an easily checked answer (when run on a known prime they should output true after their billions of calculations). They can easily be run in the background while other 'more important' tasks run, and they are usually easy to stop and restart.

George Woltman explains:

> One of the things I do is I took the guts of programmes that crunches numbers and turned it into a large number, maths package that others could use. There

have been some other projects that have used the same core routines as GIMPS. PrimeGrid, TwinPrimes, other VDC projects working with numbers.

Beyond Walls: The Research Community

Online tools are not expensive, enable sophisticated interactive training, and bring participants together in communities where they can learn from one another, and support one another's work. As a result we're seeing a great flowering of citizen science. VDC, BOINC and individual projects are transforming the concept of a research community.

The relationships that the members within each project develop are similar to the professional camaraderie that would develop between the professional scientists described above, but this community is on a much larger scale. 'There's been really an incredible amount of virtual community formation', says Dr. David Anderson, BOINC's founder and architect. 'It's clear that a lot of people are really interested in getting involved in ways other than just running software on their computer'; the community is what provides value and excitement during the running of a VDC project. These worldwide communities are each centred on the common interest of the goal or topic of a project. Whether it is an interest in searching for extraterrestrial life or a desire to contribute to the investigation of global warming, each community bonds over its common goal, through message boards, individual profiles, teams, and a credit system.

It also integrates the volunteer community with the professional scientists and computation professionals who run the project, as each depends on the others to actually do the science. This opens up the question of 'what is a science research community?' As Nielsen (2011) observed, the institutions of modern developed societies, whether governments or companies or universities, are not prepared for the new social power of individuals. People are changing faster than science. The fear of engaging with the public is not without foundation. It does require a different mindset and approach to that necessary in traditional scientific organizations 'behind walls'. Nielsen argued that in this new world universities and scientists, just as in the business world of companies and CEOs, and the world of governments and politicians, there is a need for Principal Investigators (PIs) to be publicly accountable in a way that was unnecessary in solely industrial capitalist conditions; to show authenticity, fairness, transparency and good faith. If they do not, distrust grows and they risk disastrous effect. They forego boundless free computational power. If they do engage in VDCs, but at a distance, they risk losing loyal participants, who, disaffected, will look for other projects where the scientist IS engaged, transparent and present. It calls for a humility that most scientists are not used to. Trust is built by transparency, engagement and presence. Volunteers like to see participation by the scientists on the message boards, especially communication of news such as the publication of new scientific papers based on the research of the VDC project. They want in short to be treated as a member of the research community on that project.

Research teams, like citizen groups, have been greatly democratized and enhanced by the Internet, just by virtue of the possibility of many-to-many communication. So besides the one to many dissemination of findings in journals, interaction at scientific conferences, and membership of associations with printed material disseminated, now online forums provide a constant medium for constant interaction between as many people as want to participate. Although less rich than face to face meetings, it is certainly a major improvement over the restrictions offered by the cost and professional barriers to access to journals and membership material. By allowing a higher degree of participation to larger numbers of people than was previously possible, online forums enable associations to attract and keep larger numbers of committed members than would otherwise be possible (other things being equal). Besides being free from restrictions of space, VDC communities are freer from constraints of time. Communciation in online forums does not require close synchronization between participants, so it is much easier for large numbers of people to participate. It brings greater continuity between associations by allowing discussions to continue during interludes between face to face meetings which are not uncommon among VDC but not also necessary for reinforcing morale and solidarity. GIMPS members express a very high level of morale and solidarity and most have never met each other and do not feel the need to.

Research communities that include VDC forums also reduce the high costs of coordination; instead of rearranging their schedules to attend a group meeting, they can read others' messages at their convenience. Because communication is text based, participants can quickly scan communications to eliminate those with little content and to focus on messages they consider more important. They can access information sources previously available only through libraries or not at all.

Participation in a forum consumes less of each participant's limited resources. It can also increase responsiveness. The same flexibility that computerization brought to industry (Piore and Sabel, 1994) can now be realized by associations, such as project teams and communities, with the result that there is often a fast response to emerging issues or projects.

As Klein (1999) observed, the Internet provides new means of achieving the many-to-many communications of a forum. The Internet has fewer barriers of space, time and cost than a town hall meeting. Compared to a newspaper, the Internet allows for far greater participation in many-to-many communications. By providing a new technology for forums, the Internet opens new possibilities for inclusiveness in research communities.

Concerns from the Established Institution of Science

The scientists involved in VDC recognize that some of the concerns of other scientists reluctant to get involved have merit. But their response is that those concerns can be addressed. One simple concern was the motivation and computational ability of volunteers to see a Work Unit that takes many hours or days through to the end, without turning off the machine and rendering the incomplete work unit useless. Many scientific applications were meant to be run continuously from 'start to finish' with job submission by researchers who patiently await the results on a time-shared system, and who do not interrupt the task. In VDC, user intervention, system crashes and other factors may require a task to be paused, stopped, or removed from memory and later restarted. Such a concern in ClimatePrediction.net was solved by 'Checkpointing' (Christensen et al., 2005), i.e. checkpoint time-consuming tasks (e.g. greater than an hour of runtime) and this enables a restart of the task with little loss of previously computed work. On ClimatePrediction.net this is every 15 minutes, which means that at most 15 minutes of CPU (central processing unit) time is lost when the user stops the model or shuts down the computer.

The stable and tested BOINC infrastructure has also persuaded many scientists to try VDC. The infrastructure necessary for VDC is essentially a 'vertical application' that must handle the distribution of software and Work Units to users worldwide, the web pages they will see for their work statistics, and the network communications between the users and projects servers. The software must be able to run on all hardware and software platforms. BOINC now encapsulates all aspects of the 'vertical application' required for VDC. This includes the client-side software APIs, that can be added to the scientific code, server-side work unit delivery and result uploading code, the database (mySQL), and the user and project maintenance web pages. This enables the production of a more stable volunteer computing application, which has reassured many potential scientists in their decision to use VDC (Christensen, 2005).

For ClimatePrediction.net, using the BOINC framework lead to a much higher completion rate of models finished, and a higher retention rate of volunteers, especially in the long term, with about one third of users and machines still active after six months. The original ClimatePrediction.net had a much higher attrition rate. The main reason was technical – the ClimatePrediction.net project's platform was inadequate for the variety of software configurations and machines out there (Christensen, ibid.).

With VDC you have no guarantees that the result being submitted is correct because the volunteer's computer could have certain hardware or software glitches, they could have dust in their CPU which is causing overheating and causing errors, and there is no guarantee on how long it will take for the result to come back to you. The computer can be an old, slow one or a new, fast one. The control conditions of computation are not there. The solution is to send the problem or work unit out twice or thrice and if the results are matching you can say with some degree of certainty that the answer was reliable. If the answers do not match, it is sent out again until a matching answer is returned.

In conclusion, science as a field is facing challenges of heavier computation demands, resistance to the cost barriers of access to journals and information, and the desire of ordinary people to get involved. The Internet has removed much of the barriers to involvement in science that existed under industrial capitalism, but of course, the need for accreditation and rigorous adherence to scientific norms and standards still apply. The response is the emergence of citizen science endeavours such as Voluntary Distributed Computing, where ordinary individuals can get involved, unused resources are tapped, but scientists still play a crucial leadership and validating role. The challenges and institutional responses are most obvious in the areas of science where computation is central, but similar challenges are also emerging in other areas of previously closed off institutions.

Chapter 4
Communities in Voluntary Distributed Computing

It is apparent that Voluntary Distributed Computing is far from a solitary pursuit. Instead, it is one that necessitates collective behaviour, including competition with other volunteers, both in the project itself and in the greater VDC universe. This challenges the perception of VDC as involving isolated individuals downloading software to use up their idle PC cycles, with no contact with other people doing something similar. In fact, involvement in VDC is leading to unlikely and unusual collaborations involving volunteers who are simultaneously building communities and engaging in competition with other volunteers and groups of volunteers.

Communities are central to VDC and are key to its continued growth and success. Millions of individuals do connect to projects, download the software, run it and have no contact with any other volunteer. Millions of others download the software, run it and check the website for news about the project, thereby linking in, albeit as a 'lurker' to the community infrastructure of the project. Millions more download the software, run it, and read and participate in forums with other volunteers, mostly about the project but also about life in general, with some forums having participants of ten or more years duration, as old as the project. Some of these millions join with other volunteers to form teams to compete in the ongoing quest to be the top contributors to a project, and monitor their progress, discuss tactics, celebrate together, advise and generally be a community, there to give and receive practical and emotional support.

Thus, the implications of the 'public computing' paradigm are social as well as scientific. It provides a basis for global communities centred around common interests and goals (Anderson, 2003). The changes that brought VDC about – the development of information and communication technologies to the point that one third of the world's population is connected to the Internet in 2011 with that percentage increasing exponentially every year – has enormous social ramifications. The whole notion of what is a 'community' is once again under scrutiny, and VDC provides evidence that online communities are a vital part of many people's overall sense of community.

Community

Technically, communities in general are formed when three or more people become socially connected in a generally structured or patterned way, develop a collective identity and purpose, and share an extra-dyadic 'sense' of belonging to a social entity larger than the individual or dyad. More colloquially, communities provide a sense of belonging, of connection, a source and destination for practical and emotional help, a sense of obligation and responsibility, regular contact and a feeling of reciprocity.

The Internet has reinvigorated both the concept and practice of 'community'. For the first time people with shared interests or emotional connections can connect without limits of time or space (Rheingold, 2000). However, 'community' is a term that is much used and abused, with debates about the demise or growth of it generating discussion as long as there have been human collectivities, and the key points in that debate are worth repeating here in considering the communities that are part of VDC.

Sociologists have long expressed fears that rapid modernization means the loss of community, leaving a handful of transitory, disconnected, weakly supportive relationships. Indeed, sociologists since the advent of the industrial revolution and the first massive movement of people into urban areas have beaten their breasts over what this is doing to 'community'. The keynote was set by Ferdinand Tönnies (1887) who claimed there were fundamental differences between the communally-organized societies of yesteryear (which he called *gemeinschaft*) and the contractually-organized societies *(gesellschaft)* associated with the coming of the Industrial Revolution. Tönnies asserted that communally-organized societies, supposedly characteristic of rural areas and underdeveloped societies, would have densely-interconnected social relationships composed principally of neighbours and kin. Community was rural, bounded geographically and life-long.

By contrast, Tönnies asserted that contractually-organized societies, supposedly characteristic of industrial cities, would have more sparsely-knit relationships composed principally of ties between friends and acquaintances, rather than relatives or neighbors. He believed that the lack of cohesion in such *gesellschaft* societies was leading to specialized, contractual exchanges replacing communally-enforced norms of mutual support.

Karl Marx (1852), Friedrich Engels' (1885) and Simmel (1922) all worried that industrial capitalism had created new types of interpersonal exploitation that drove people apart, resulting in the loss of community. Although sociologist Max Weber (1946; 1958) extolled modern rationality, he also feared that bureaucratization and urbanization were weakening communal bonds and traditional authority. Sociologist Émile Durkheim (1897) feared that the loss of solidarity had weakened communal support and fostered social pathology. A generation later, sociologist Georg Simmel (1922) celebrated urban liberation but also worried that the new individualism would lead to superficial relationships.

On the other hand, many of the same commentators noted that the large-scale reorganization of production had created new opportunities for community relations (echoing what the organizational changes wrought by the Internet are doing two centuries later). Weber argued that bureaucracy and urbanization would liberate many from the traditional, stultifying bases of community, and Durkheim

(1893) argued that the new complex divisions of labour were binding people together in networks of interdependent 'organic solidarity'. In the same article that he worried about the consequences of urban liberation, Simmel argued that in the new cities, individuals were no longer totally enmeshed in one social circle. Therefore, they would have greater personal freedom as they manouvered through their partial social attachments.

The debate on whether community was alive and well or a lamented lost ideal continued throughout the twentieth century, as social scientists in the new North American world adapted Tönnies' concerns, debating whether modern times occasioned the loss of in developed Western societies (e.g., Berger 1960; Gans 1962; Gans 1967; Grant 1969; Nisbet 1962; Parsons 1943; Slater 1970; Stein 1960).

Most recently and with huge popular attention, Robert Putnam in *Bowling Alone* (2001) lamented the decline in community in the United States. He argued that Americans used to bowl in leagues together, usually after work, but no more. For him, this symbolized how Americans have become increasingly disconnected from one another and how social structures – be they church or political parties – have disintegrated leading to a crisis of community. He cites the reasons as: increased pressures of time and money, sprawl and suburbanization, increased television watching, and a generational divide.

Putnam's characterizations of community as based on political, religious, and community based civic associations continues Tönnies understanding of community as bound by physical space. However, the measure differs. Rather than kin or immediate neighbours, Putnam uses a person's civic associations as an estimate of that person's social connectedness. The more meetings you attend, clubs you join, the more connected you are.

This conception of community as based on a common physical space is one that echoes the pastoral ideal, the passing of which preoccupied Tönnies so much. However, there are strong grounds for seeing that pastoral idyll as an ideal that never actually existed in pure form. Wellman (1999) points out that pre-industrially, many villages were not a solidary village – ties regularly went beyond the village boundaries. Various factions competed within the village for wealth and status. Each faction used their ties outside the village to enhance their local standing, and each used their local support to build external alliances. Also, contrary to contemporary pastoralist myth of immutable villages, many families were socially and spatially mobile. They often worked in the city when they were young adults, but retained ties with their rural villages. Artisans and soldiers were frequently on the road. Women married and moved, geographically and socially. Servants' ties to their distant families concurrently linked their masters' families to the servants' rural home.

The preoccupation with physical co-location does not fit with the reality of modern societies. Most contemporary Western communities do not resemble preindustrial villages for they are socially diverse, sparsely knit and well-connected to the outside world. These are only partial communities that do not command a person's full allegiance. Rather, each person is a limited member of multiple communities such as kinship groups, neighbourhoods and friendship circles. Hence, Putnam's emphasis on the importance of civic associations and his fears for community in the face of their decline.

Networks

Wellman and Gulia (1999) argue that Putnam's fears have much less power when you consider community not as something that must occupy the same limited physical space, but rather as a collection of social ties that are not limited by space. With the rise in awareness of networks both in theory (Granovetter, 1985; Powell, 1990; Watts, 2004; Porter and Powell, 2006; Barabasi, 2003; Holton, 2005) and practice (Keck and Sikkink, 1996; DeTona and Lentin, 2007; Holohan, 2005), there is a realization that neighbourhood and kinship ties are only a portion of people's overall community networks because cars, planes and phones can maintain relationships over long distance. Communities do not have to be solidary groups of densely knit neighbours but can also exist as social networks of kin, friends, and workmates who do not necessarily live in the same neighbourhoods. There has been a move from defining community in terms of physical space to defining it in terms of social networks.

John, a volunteer on several VDC projects put it thus: 'if you live in a small community or in an estate in west Dublin and there's 1000 people in it, the chances are you're not going to bump into somebody else who's into scientific computing in your housing estate. But there may be millions of people around the world who are in to that thing. The internet allows these communities to exist that couldn't exist before because of the distances across the planet'.

An understanding of the world as individuals connected through networks (as well as being members of primary groups such as the family and secondary groups such as work organizations) has been there for several decades (Granovetter, 1973; 1974) but with the development of information and communication technologies has taken on new possibilities and ramifications (Watts, ibid.). The network approach allows analysts to go looking for social relationships that transcend groups or localities. A group is only a special type of social network, one that is densely-knit (most people are directly connected) and tightly-bounded (most relations stay within the same set of people). To be sure, there are densely-knit and tightly-bounded work groups and community groups. Yet there are other kinds of work and community networks whose relationships are sparsely-knit with only a minority of members of the workplace or community directly connected with each other.

By using the social network approach, analysts discovered that community had not disappeared. Instead, community had moved out of its traditional neighbourhood base as the constraints of space weakened. This shift in perspective from neighbourhood community to community network allows us to see the extent to which large-scale social changes have created new forms of association and altered traditional kinship and neighbouring structures.

Community and the Internet

The early utopian claims for the Internet 'solving' the alleged community crisis first of all made the same mistake of accepting the pastoral physical ideal as the actual standard. Secondly it made the same mistake of being parochial – it treated the Internet as an isolated social phenomenon without taking into account how interactions on the Internet fit with other aspects of people's lives. But now it is becoming apparent that virtual communities can strengthen the weakened real-world social network. The Internet is only one of many ways in which the same people interact. It is not a separate reality. People bring to their online interactions such baggage as their gender, stage in the life-cycle, cultural milieu, socioeconomic status, and offline connections with others. People involved in virtual communities know that computer networks are also social networks. VDC is one part of a person's rich, interconnected online/offline interaction. The richness of civic associations, such as the communities around VDC, present a strong rebuttal to Putnam's theory about the decline of civic associations in that it provides evidence for people's desire for community but also provides evidence of the diverse sources of that sense of community and connection.

For instance, the sub-community of approximately 20 moderators (at any one time) in ClimatePrediction.net, spans the globe: geographically they include moderators North-West of the United States, mid-West USA, UK, Ireland, Australia, Finland, New Zealand. In common with many other Internet-based communities around the world, the moderators have never met as a group, although they communicate with each other constantly over email, and via forum messages, chat and sometimes telephone. The community provides a sense of belonging, of connection, a source and destination for practical and emotional help, a sense of obligation and responsibility, regular contact and a feeling of reciprocity. In short, they are a virtual community.

Jim, one of the moderators based in the North-West of the US, said:

> The British have a term "mate" and we have a term here "buddy" and I think it's on that level. We get along ok, we're scattered across the world. There's a few in England, Wales and Scotland, who have met, but most of us have never met and never will. We know each other's names, we write regular emails back and forth, two of us used to be weather forecasters so we have that in common, and we all have an interest in this project in common. We all have some affinity for being of assistance to other people.

The emotional importance of his involvement was brought home to him when he was suddenly several days with no access to the forum.

> We had a big storm here a few years ago, we were without electricity here for
> 5 and a half days. It was a very cold time, the winds were hurricane force and
> basically all I could do was stay in bed most of this time and try to stay warm.
> That's my experience in the interim since I've been doing this where I've been
> outside of it for that long, involuntarily. I'd have to come up with something
> else, start writing again, if I didn't have this.

But do these online communities have the emotional intensity, levels of trust,
reciprocity, of real-world communities? Putnam noticed that the Internet enables
individuals who share very specific interests to find each other and communicate.
Computer mediated interactions are more egalitarian and cost effective over long
distances. But he worried that the loss of non-verbal information normally present
in face to face conversations makes computer chat less robust, leading to decreases
in trust, reciprocity, and solidarity. The bottom line for Putnam was that our real
world communities are suffering from dwindling social connection, and that the
virtual communities currently available are not suitable replacements.

Other critics worry that life on the Internet can never be meaningful or complete
because it will lead people away from the full range of in-person contact. Or that
people will become so engrossed that they will lose contact with 'real life'.

In fact, what Putnam is seeking is actually a by-product of the activity of doing
the work on VDC projects and engaging in discussion with fellow project or team
members. The volunteering of time and money by individuals and organizations
is widely seen as forming the basis for civil society – the web of voluntary
associations and social movements in which people engage in collective action to
provide services and influence public policy or standards of social life (Cohen and
Arato, 1992). With its ability to put information power in the hands of the people,
the Internet, in particular online forums, holds the promise for wider and more
effective citizen participation in public affairs (Klein, 1999).

The VDC community has two strong elements. One part is driven primarily
by credits and the competitive element, with the community aspect of the teams
and forums organized around this. The other part is driven primarily by the
'science' or the 'ethics' of contributing to work on mitigating the impact of climate
change for example, or to the efforts of finding a vaccine for malaria. Those VDC
participants embody what Bennett (2007) calls the 'actualizing citizen', one who
learns to practice a more personal politics that is less oriented toward influencing
government and more towards community service and informal participation in
social movement activism that targets a broad range of institutions. He cautions
that both the older 'dutiful citizen' model and the newer 'actualizing citizen' model
have something to offer and can learn from each other. The dutiful citizen can
see new opportunities for engagement through digital media and unconventional
associations, and the 'actualizing citizen' needs access to the conventional civic and
political worlds to realize their values and goals (Bennett, 2007: 10).

This is particularly the case if one takes a broad or expanded view of civic life
(Levine, 2007), not focusing on electoral participation, government service, the

organization and workings of government and political activism, but rather on the governing of the commons, or the negotiation of laws and social norms (such as volunteering), efforts to build cultural and political understanding or harmony across social groups, and media literacy and media production oriented towards public affairs.

Whatever their motivation, the community they are part of on VDC plays a very strong part in the retention of a significant number of volunteers.

VDC as a Community

Let us consider the elements of 'community' and the degree to which VDC contains those elements – a sense of belonging, of connection, a source and destination for practical and emotional help, a sense of obligation and responsibility, regular contact and a feeling of reciprocity.

Certainly, the structure – the communal meeting place that connects people and allows for regular contact – is there through the forums and message boards that go with each project. The most common access to community for people in VDC is through BOINC. Each BOINC project is given a website template to create the communities; so one will find a home page, a message board, and a credit system that is the basis for user and team leader boards for any BOINC project. On the message board, individuals are able to discuss whatever interests them, such as questions about the projects, the science behind the particular topic, or interesting results they have encountered.

Because the projects have large numbers of participants (for example, SETI@ home has about 135,000 active users), the community relies on the messages boards to break the group down by subinterests; examples of sub-interests include common nationality or a common reason for joining the project. The sub-communities' significantly smaller size in turn makes individual relationships more of a reality. For example, language-specific communities as well as national communities have developed their own sites and message boards similar to that of the worldwide project page.

Leader boards organized by individual, computer, and team are displayed prominently on the front page of each project, illustrating their importance in the sub-community. A user's relative position on the boards is based upon the number of credits that a cruncher obtains. Credits are awarded for each work unit processed on the user's computer; so, the greater the contribution to the project, the more credits one can receive. Credits serve as the fuel for the communities by sparking the natural spirit of competition. With that competition, a sort of social hierarchy develops, where the amount of respect a member of the community receives is proportional to the amount of credits he or she has earned. A large number of credits elicits a correspondingly large number of responses to message board posts.

The common interest is a central tie for most people in VDC. A virtual community can be seen as a group in which individuals come together around a shared purpose, interest, or goal (Jooh Ko et al., 2007). Most depend on electronic communications to support interaction among members who are not physically co-located. Typical computer-mediated community interaction, just as with ClimatePrediction.net and the other projects, includes news and information sharing, problem solving (such as Q and A, FAQs, best practices and discussions) and routine communication (such as email and chat). Most activity takes the form of posting or viewing opinions, questions, information, and knowledge within the community's message boards. Consequently, posting and viewing are fundamental elements in the ongoing life of VDC, as in any virtual community. In any given community, the posting activity stimulant is not the same as the viewing activity stimulant. While viewing activity is associated with the perception by community members of community usefulness, posting activity is influenced by offline interaction and the quality of the IT infrastructure (Jooh Ko et al., ibid.).

Contrary to Putnam and other critics, strong ties that are online have many characteristics that are similar to strong offline ties. They encourage frequent, companionable contact and are voluntary. They facilitate reciprocal, mutual support of the tie partners' needs. Moreover, the placelessness of email contact aids long-term contact, without the loss of the tie that so often accompanies geographical mobility. Walther (1995) says intimacy is possible, just slower than face to face. That is more likely to happen for those involved in the same projects and same forums over a long period of time, such as the Mersenne Forum of the GIMPS project. There are also many online interactions of those that see it as 'intimate secondary relationships': informal, frequent and supportive community ties that nevertheless operate only in one specialized domain.

The Internet, and VDC, can provide emotional support, giving a sense of belonging through meeting like-minded people, thus reducing loneliness, overcoming geographical or social isolation or isolating personal circumstances (such as being separated from a former spouse, and not seeing much of one's child in the case of a volunteer involved in several projects).

For many who are geographically and socially isolated, it provides a link into an alternative world to their surroundings and exposes them to people and views outside their usual social milieu, but yet who they connect with.

For Mike Vang, the founder of the Mersenne Forum in GIMPS, VDC gives him an entree point into a global community and a very different milieu from his offline world.

> I was in the military; I was in the first Gulf War and Somalia, so I have some military experience for the national good. It's where my peace testimony comes from, from seeing the bad crime. On the forum, I'm surrounded by all these people who are from around the world, people in India, Korea, Africa, people in Italy for a while. We share so many common interests, bicycling, the outdoors. But if you go onto a regular or larger forum that I've ever been on, it's always "hey USA we're no 1". I was born and raised in a little town and I've been around the world in the army but never experienced other cultures other than the

Internet. For me it's like I don't know if I'll get a chance to go visit, it's really only through other people. So when for instance, Garo told me he was in the mountains of Italy, riding his bicycle up and down these famous mountain, I was like, wow, tell me about it. I was like, I'm living by proxy, I'm living these experiences. The problem for me is as I've indicated I'm a red neck from Ohio who married young, but is now being able to hang out with people who are mensa level people. There is of course the learning curve, you just don't jump in there and start posting. You know people do sometimes they go on a forum and just register join a project and start asking questions about research and stuff. I've learned that people in the forums are not just resources, they're resources and people that are to be valued.

People in real life get all kinds of support from community members but they have to turn to different ones for different kinds of help. This means that people must maintain differentiated portfolios of ties to obtain a variety of resources. VDC allows this, facilitating finding out information as much as providing social connection. Forums also provide a place to assist newcomers to the project, or others seeking assistance with problems in running the project.

VDC volunteers are notable for their willingness to communicate with strangers online and this contrasts with in-person situations where bystanders are often reluctant to intervene and help strangers. Yet bystanders are more apt to intervene when they are the only ones around, and requests are read by solitary individuals, alone at their screens. As far as the recipient knows, he or she may be the only one who could provide help, so they do so. The willingness to communicate with strangers is indicated by the fact that in most forums, moderators do not have to coordinate – there is always enough people online to help with queries.

Norms of reciprocity work in VDC too. Those who have been helped are very willing to help in turn. Many of the exchanges that take place online are between persons who have never met face to face, have only weak ties, and are not bound into densely knit community structures that could enforce norms of reciprocity. Nevertheless, many Net members do reciprocate support, even to weak ties. Many volunteers (as they gain more experience with the project's computing or scientific aspects) are happy to act as 'gurus' or 'moderators' to the larger community.

> I do a great deal to support and encourage members in their DC efforts by offering instruction and advice. Being in the training field in my line of work, this comes natural to me. This makes it akin to my work relationships. Even so, any time you get a team working well together, there is a bonding that takes place and you take interest in how others are doing (Volunteer on several projects).

One particular strength of VDC is that the accumulation of small, individual acts can sustain a large community because each act *is seen by the entire group* and this helps to perpetuate an image of generalized reciprocity and mutual aid. There are also archives of the discussion threads – you can see a history of interaction.

Reciprocity and helping neighbours in the community is clearly present. For the small core of enthusiasts, involvement has a spin-off pattern. Most of the respondents in the Holohan and Garg 2005 study, (74 per cent), participated in more than one project at one point or another. However, 56 per cent were running only one project at that point in time. The usual pattern seemed to be of participants being interested in one project and starting with just one. As they participated more actively in the forums, they became aware of the existence of more projects and started trying them out. The reasons for this diversification are many. Sometimes, the project they started on comes to an end. Sometimes, they 'helped out' by participating in a project to help their team or organization improve its standings in the statistics.

The sense of community is important for attracting and retaining volunteers. Barry Wellman has noted: 'Communities are networks of interpersonal ties that provide sociability, support, information, a sense of belonging and social identity' (2001:1). As one participant in a forum on ArsTechnica put it: 'Team Vodka Martini became my home'. This is in spite of the fact that the majority have never met the other people they work with on VDC projects (Holohan and Garg, 2005). They do however, spend a lot of time online with each other, with 47 per cent of respondents to one study citing between ten minutes and an hour of activity daily, and 31 per cent more than one hour daily (Holohan and Garg, ibid.).

For many, it is an intrinsic part of the social, if not emotional, landscape of their lives, but rarely the main source of connection. Many in the surveys liken it to a community of work colleagues or sports buddies. Holohan and Garg (2005) reported that when respondents were asked how they viewed their relationship with other members of the distributed computing community, 39 per cent of the respondents classified them as casual friends and 14 per cent as close friends with a further 25 per cent as acquaintances and 11 per cent each as work colleagues and strangers.

Work has changed with many people no longer tied to specific office locations. For those people who work at home, the constant presence of a VDC forum which they are part of, particularly when it contains other like-minded people, provides a virtual sense of collegiality. They also incorporate their responses on the forums into their work day, work and play segueing into each other smoothly. Chris, a volunteer for GIMPS said: 'I have 25 screens which have my various projects on them. One of my screens is devoted to the Mersenne forum site, where I drop in, see what people are chatting about, keeping track of what is the buzz currently going on'.

Like Minded People or 'Mental Networks'

However, the dominant and defining characteristic of what connected respondents and interviewees to others in VDC was 'like-mindedness'. Chayko (2002) noted that virtual communities differ from 'real-life' communities in the *basis* upon

Table 4.1   Social and Emotional Life of Volunteers: Sample of responses from the 2010-2011 survey on the role that VDC plays in volunteers' social and emotional life

Part of the overall community involvement for multiple areas of my life. e.g. I count the time spent as the same value equivalent to the time spent in volunteering at local k-* school. I try to roll the VDC knowledge gained into topics and talks at the school.

Online VDC friends can never replace the offline relationships, but are for sure a nice addition to life.

Online acquaintances are my 2nd most common communication behind work. But it is shallow for the most part. I have a couple close friends that I consult on the big issues.

My feelings for my friends involved with F@H are like any other friendships would be. We do share our life's burdens and concerns with each other. We communicate amongst each other, almost daily and we strengthen each other through this bond.

I feel like my real family is online.

They are completely separate. I would not turn to the VDC'ers for anything other than computer related advice. There is little emotional tie to the VDC'ers.

Feeling of general camaraderie, much like members of a sports team. Not really what I would consider friends necessarily, but more than just acquaintances. My DC relationships tend to be separated from personal ones, don't involve nearly as much time.

I regard the online VDC community as independent of my friends and colleagues who live in my country. With the VDC community the communication is not personal, more like a teaching/learning environment.

I just let my laptop run the data.

which participants perceive their relationships to be intimate. People on the Internet have a greater tendency to develop feelings of closeness on the basis of shared interests rather than on the basis of shared social characteristics such as gender and socioeconomic status. So they are relatively homogenous in their interests and attitudes. In many virtual communities, members are relatively heterogenous in the participants' age, social class, ethnicity, life-cycle stage and other aspects of their social backgrounds. The exception for VDC is gender, with the majority of participants, at least the majority of the participants in teams and forums, being male.

Emile Durkheim described how social contact that is primarily based on daily face to face contact or sporadic communication (usually by letter historically), produces a shared set of values and norms and resulting solidarity that is 'mechanical'. This however sacrificed individuality to the group. After the industrial revolution and with the urbanization of society, social relations tended to depend more on the sharing of 'common ideas, interests, sentiments, and occupations' than on the sharing of literal space (Durkheim 1984 [1893]: xlii) producing what he called an 'organic solidarity'. ICTs are now playing a large part in the discovery and development of interpersonal commonalities across space and time. They have permitted people to 'see' and know of – and thus potentially feel connected to – many more people than before, but crucially based on common interests and like-mindedness. This interdependence on others who live great distances away and will probably never be met can be thought of as a new kind of 'organic' solidarity (see Durkheim 1984 [1893]).

The bonds that are created in virtual communities such as VDC are not usually generated or maintained by face to face contact and so exist primarily in a mental realm, a space that is not created solely in the imagination of one individual but requires two or more minds – a 'meeting of the minds' – to make possible, to 'activate'. These bonds are sociomental (Zerubavel, 1993). They are the manifestation of an absolutely genuine and often deeply felt sense of connection; that while the physical distance separating people may be great, the social distance between them may be very small indeed. The portion of sociomental space in which people are brought together via computer has been termed cyberspace by writer William Gibson (1995).

How does this happen? People in common, inhabited social territory, whether it be cultures, subcultures, or groups, construct mental models together. In using similar mental models in generally similar ways, people in a group or a thought collective or a culture go on to construct a world together that comes to be seen as a 'natural fact' and is full of meaning for those involved. In fact, they have constructed what the anthropologist Clifford Geertz (1977) termed an 'imaginative universe', one that is shared mentally, in the imagination.

The 'imaginative universe' helps structure, order, and process the thoughts of those involved in it and it is in thinking similarly to others in this structured and modelled way that we can mentally connect with others without the absolute necessity of face to face contact. It can produce the feelings of like-mindedness and resonance so critical to the development of social connectedness.

Chayko (ibid.) notes that when a sociomental connection gains strength and durability, it can be considered a bond, and when it encompasses three or more people, a community of the mind can form. Long before the emergence of information and communication technologies, in the first decades of the twentieth century, the sociologist George Herbert Mead argued that even people who do not physically meet can serve as 'abstract' social groups that influence people and inspire the formation of 'definite' social relations among members (1934: 157). Communities of the mind yield networks of sociomental connections and bonds that are mental rather than physical (mental networks) but provide a sense of structure, identity, purpose, and belonging for their members.

As with offline communities, people come and go, and every so often a round of introductions will be held. One taken from a thread on the Mersenne forum below shows the interaction of individual volunteers and the aspects of themselves that they list and to which others respond. Although giving personal information, their common interest in VDC takes up the most space. It can be overwhelming to join an up and running community, or for people who have been around for a while but not that active to say more about themselves, and cognizant of that, some senior members initiate ways to have online welcome sessions. One such example was a 'Hello – Nice to Meet You' Thread on the Mersenne forum.

Nineteen people responded and of those who identified where they were physically, they came from Greenwich in the UK; 'Cowtown', Texas, USA; Italy; Zagreb, Croatia; Quebec, Canada; California, USA; Hong Kong; Sweden; Upstate New York, USA; San Francisco, USA; Siberia, Russia; Michigan, USA; Wisconsin, USA and Cambridge, UK. The information they posted contained a mixture of demographic and personal information, detail about their technological ability and humorous observations. On the demographic side, one poster started with '36.03 and married with 2 boys, 2.02 and 3.10 years old, the older one with a definite affinity for numbers', another said 'I am an old man of 50...and operate a train for Bay Area Rapid Transit'; 'I am a high school senior in Hong Kong. My dream (at the moment) is to get into Caltech'. 'I work for a Brick company and since the construction industry slows down in the winter I always get laid off 3 months. This gives me plenty of time to do math research'.

Technologically, they indicate the time they have been active in VDC, what machines they use and what they are particularly interested in. Responses include beginners:

> I installed Prime95 a few weeks ago and am currently working on my first candidate: $(2^{20221283})-1$. It is 83.53% done now, but that will probably change by the time this post is read. I am only running the program on one computer at the moment, but its a powerful one: 3.055GHz.

> Newsflash!
> Yesterday afternoon (local time, +1 GMT) the GIMPS-project got another processor to aid in the noble quest for larger prime-numbers. The processor, a P4 2.4Ghz, lives in the south of sweden with her owner Robin Karlsson, 18 years old. When she don't process webpages for her master to browse or games for her master to play she has previously spent her time idleing. But not anymore. From now on she will do whatever work the PrimeNet server tells her to instead of just wasting CPU-cycles.

> [Head of a National VDC Team]Today we passed 1000 LL P90 CPU years, but apart from a deep interest in Number Theory I look pretty normal...My own machines are hidden behind my desk; I use them via RealVNC so you can see only one Keyboard, Mouse and Video on it. We actually run 44 different boxen, both at home and remotely. Oh yes...it's fine to have so many friends...as long as they accept to be borged.

Amidst the introductory notes, the use of the word 'boxen' opened up an exchange. A poster wrote: 'You don't say boxes?' Another poster jumped in and replied 'For anyone whose mother tongue isn't English, "boxen" is just humor. The correct plural is obviously "boxes"'. The original poster of 'boxen' responded with a *blushing* and continued to poke fun at the use of 'forums' when it should be 'fora'. 'Shame on me, I read '-en' instead of '-es' so many times in these fora (plural of forum, from latin:-DDD) that I didn't even thought it could be misunderstood...signs off (that laughs and learns from every bit of information)'.

Paul, a volunteer in GIMPS, said what keeps him coming back is 'the chatting and collaboration with other like minded people. There's quite a wide variety of people there many of whom are very smart. I like talking and working with smart people. It stops my, helps stop my own brain from seizing up...[the forums] play a critical role in that it allows like minded people to get together and talk about their obsession'.

Many of the survey respondents and interviewees stated that without the Internet, and VDC, that it would be difficult for them to find 'like-minded' people. Paul says:

> I actually speak with people relatively little face to face; my field is very much a minority interest. I don't know how many people are active on the forum, but I think there is a few hundred worldwide, I'd say at most. Only some of them would I actually regard as being professional mathematicians and scientists, you know, people who could make a living doing research in those fields. There certainly are some people there but in the forum there's I don't know twenty or so scattered throughout the entire world. Now not everybody who is active in this business is on the forum. So it's the interest of a small number of geeks spread throughout the world. It's actually quite unusual to find two people with the same interests anywhere near each other, unless they happen to be working in the same circle. And in my case I know precisely one other person in Cambridge who does this sort of thing. I think I'm trying to think where the next nearest might be one could be, guy I communicate with. It's probably in Dublin.

As Paul points out, not everyone who is active in the project is active on the forum, but the forums are used sporadically by some and read or perused by others, neither of which precludes the people doing so from feeling a connection or being part of the community. As Jooh Ko (2007) states: 'Most activity takes the form of posting or viewing opinions, questions, information, and knowledge within the community's message boards. Consequently, posting and viewing are fundamental elements in the ongoing life of any virtual community'. Jooh Ko does not discount those who only view from being part of the community.

As Max Weber explains: The anticipation of the existence of another person – or becoming oriented toward an 'other' – is a distinctly social act,

> Social action, which includes both failure to act and passive acquiescence, may be oriented to the past, present, or expected behavior of others (1978: 22).

As we become oriented toward others' behaviour, whether these others are formally 'known' to us or not, we actually engage in a type of social action. When we project ourselves mentally into a situation, we really experience it (Goffman, 1974: 381). So people who are on VDC project websites but yet do not participate are still interacting in a socially meaningful way.

> John, a volunteer in several projects and living in Ireland, tracks the long term and highest contributors from Ireland and notes that several have no contact with any other person doing VDC, but they are listed on the ranks of their chosen projects. He has tried unsuccessfully to recruit them to the Paddys in Space team. He says: 'There is one particular very big player a guy over in [town in West of Ireland], he has a bank of computers he's always been up near the top...I managed to track down the guy and I got his phone number and I rang him. He's a very quiet man he doesn't communicate on forums and he doesn't want to know about anybody else but he likes to be the most powerful person in the country computer wise. He buys more and more computers but he does it on his own, he stacks up banks of computers but doesn't want to chat with anyone.

VDC volunteers emphasize that meaningful contact is indeed possible via the communities around the projects they are participating in. In fact, among the German SETI@home community, which regularly meets face to face, there have been three marriages in recent years.

Cliques and Communities

Communities generate social capital and VDC is no exception. 'Social capital' (Granovetter, 1974; 1973; 1985), by analogy with notions of physical capital and human capital, is the idea that social networks have value. Whereas physical capital refers to physical objects and human capital refers to properties of individuals, social capital refers to connections among individuals – social networks and the norms of reciprocity and trustworthiness that arise from them. People are embedded in a dense network of reciprocal social relations.

People who have a lot of weak links, are bridges or connectors have: rich social capital – this is what you can call having lots of connections. If you need to receive or send information or want to exert influence you are more likely to be successful if you are in the position of a bridge or connector. But social capital can come in two forms: networks or clique capital.

Bridging (inclusive) social capital is outward looking and encompasses people across diverse social cleavages, for instance in the civil rights movement and ecumenical religious organizations. It is good for linkage to external assets and for information diffusion. So the VDC ArsTechnica forum's team recruits new volunteers from a variety of projects; there is active 'head-hunting' with high performers being invited to join projects that might be of interest to them. Bridging capital can also generate broader identities and reciprocity (the ArsTechnica 'flying squads' sent out to help teams that were slipping down the rankings), whereas bonding capital bolsters narrower selves, so intense allegiance characterizes particular project specific forums, such as GIMPS' Mersenne forum.

Although in theory VDC is based on community of common interests, in practice the majority of participants are male and technologically oriented if not experienced. Although some are aware of this (Bruce Allen of Einstein@home, Carl Christensen of ClimatePrediction.net, Dave Anderson of BOINC) as something that needs to be broadened out, the bonding social capital that is currently generated can exclude female volunteers and those from non-technical backgrounds. One volunteer who was both female and non-technical in background, but who quickly become an avid contributor in terms of numbers crunched and discussion in forums found that there was no way to describe the opposition to her but as a form of sexism and a product of a culture that can turn projects into male, 'techie' domains.

Anna recalls:

> There were other moderators who were obviously quite cross at having a person who was "non-techie" around. And they, on a couple of occasions, there were snide comments, not just snide, they were so obvious, very unfavourable comments being made about someone being a former language teacher. Totally out of order in this day and age one cannot say this sort of thing. I don't know if I'd been a teacher of a tech subject this might not ever have arisen. It was actually useful to be there as a teacher, as amongst other things, I've put in quite a bit of help on the translation side. There were quite a lot of documents that had to be translated and I could help there...It's just pure sexism. This happened on three different occasions. Each time this happened, the first thing you have to do, in my view, is ask "have I really done anything to deserve this to be said?" Fortunately, on the forum you don't have to reply immediately, you have time to think about things, which can make a bit of a difference. Is it justified? Is it fair? So in every case I just confronted the person, but not in private, they had this publicly on the forum so I had to reply publicly on the forum. In every case, it pretty well had the desired effect, the person doing it didn't do it anymore. I tried to be very calm about it, I didn't want to sound angry, that wasn't what I wanted. I felt angry but I don't think an angry tone would...I wanted to give a reason why this sort of remark was out of order.

She clarifies why she felt there was opposition to her: 'it's far more likely on these forums that the men would be the programmers and that the women would not be the programmers. From that point of view, I think there was an element of sexism in the comments'.

Forums and Teams

Forums are the focal point of community interaction. They can be based around projects, either independent (GIMPS' Mersenne Forum) or part of the BOINC set up (CPDN forum), and they facilitate discussion between individual volunteers and also organize and facilitate team discussion. Some teams come out of interaction on forums, and some forums such as ArsTechnica, are not associated with any one project but are a forum for volunteers who can be involved in more than one project.

The power of joining a team in generating a 'community' feel is significant. Isabel, a volunteer on CPDN described how: 'I joined a team and got to know a couple of members of my team, and personally, I think that the team aspect is very important. It helps people to know each other and sometimes the teams set up their own forums. I belong to a BOINC team, and I've got to know, over the internet, two or three people on my team, and this can be very helpful to encourage people, to provide a social side to those who want to know. I think that generally speaking the people in the team, some of the teams, really, just want to know each other, be with likeminded people. But generally speaking, the teams want to do well. They want everyone in the team to be doing as much as possible'.

Teams can be based on work place affiliation, nationality, or ethnic minorities – Geraldine states: 'My own team is Catalonia [although not a Catalonian herself], which is the Spanish minority. The people who belong to it are Catalan separatists, they don't feel Spanish, they feel they are Catalans' – or esoteric bases, such as a passion for Monty Python movies – the Team that Goes 'Ni'.

What a 'community' is has changed over the years in VDC, particularly after the launch of BOINC. For pre-BOINC veterans, the sense of community has gone down because when approximately the same number of participants per team pre-BOINC are now distributed over two hundred projects, there is not going to be that many people working on the same project, so there is less to share. It is still the oldest projects, including the ones who remain outside BOINC, that have the most loyal following. On the one hand, BOINC opened up and increased participation; on the other hand, it diluted the glue that community provides.

Trust is an essential element in a community. Trust resulting from working together is called 'process based trust' (Zucker, 1987) and working together as part of the same VDC project can yield 'institutional based trust' (Zucker, ibid.). Both types of trust are reinforced greatly through the additional activity of participation in a team and in a forum. The forums are a place where there is friendly competition amongst members of a particular team as well as cooperation amongst team members in order to improve the relative standing of their own team. This structure is replicated at the team level where there is competition amongst the teams and at the same time cooperation amongst the team to help achieve the project goals. In this way, a hierarchy of interests is created with the interests of the individual, the team and the project coming into conflict and confluence at different times. The forums provide a place to discuss and analyze the performance of different teams as well as of members within a team. All the techniques to improve performance are shared with everyone on the forum which in the case of ArsTechnica and Free-DC are all members of the same team and in the case of the Mersenne Forum with people from diverse teams. This sharing evolves into a sense of community. This sense of community in turn reinforces competition within teams and between teams.

Case Study: The Mersenne Forum

Individuals can play a transformative role in institutions at times of technologically induced change or flux (Fligstein, 2001; McAdam and Fligstein, 2012). Individuals can have a much bigger impact than under stable conditions, such as existed in the field of science during industrial capitalism before the advent of Internet related technologies. A number of the principal investigators featured in this book, such as George Woltman, the founder of GIMPS, and key system administrators are playing such a role in VDC and the transformation of computationally heavy science. But so too are some of the volunteers, and one such individual is Mike Vang, the founder of the Mersenne Forum, which is the forum for the Great Internet Mersenne Prime Search project and a very strong community forum. The focus of a significant portion of the research for this book, has this forum 'settled down to be the premier meeting place for social discussions of computational number series' (Paul) or is it 'the most intelligent, closest, silliest, definitely the longest running family [in VDC]' (Mike Vang)? Or is it both? Certainly, it is long lasting, a place of high level discussion of math, computational number series and much else, much of it learned but silly at the same time, and close – the repeated analogy is that of a family, including annoying members and ruptures but also with a strong loyalty.

What is the history of this forum? How did this particular culture emerge? What are the consequences for the project? The project clearly benefits, attracting knowledgeable participants who are dedicated to the search, many of whom are veterans of the intense days of competition in the first decade of VDC, and emerging as the most stable and enduring independent VDC project, i.e. outside the BOINC platform.

A key factor is the founder, George Woltman. Not part of the scientific establishment, Woltman is nonetheless one of the most involved Principal Investigators or equivalent, whose responsiveness and hands on involvement has been central to the appeal of the project from the start.

GIMPS was started in 1996 and was one of the projects that the ArsTechnica teams crunched for. As the projects multiplied, Mike Vang proposed to start a team that focused only on one project, GIMPS. He emailed the founder and head of GIMPS, George Woltman and suggested starting a forum for GIMPS. It slowly grew in popularity and Vang added little sub-forums such as the Lounge for hanging out in, a puzzle forum, a technology forum, a soap box, a hobbies area, and in July 2012, the Mersenne Forum celebrated its 10th anniversary. Once he started the forum, Vang handed over leadership of the team he had been on to someone else and concentrated on building up the forum. From then to time of publication (2013), he hosts the forum on his own web server, paying hosting fees and being responsible for its existence.

He recalls his considerations in building it up:

> you have to create an environment where people want to talk about themselves and want to feel like they're different. So we created like a mob persona where I was kind of like the Godfather and Digital Concepts and the other guys would be part of this silly little structure. Everyone had a place inside that structure and I didn't have to do anything once it was set up.

Initially the forum was aimed at what Vang calls the 'the geeks, a person who likes you know, movies and technology and computers. But they don't want to get into the maths, they're not truly nerds, just geeks you know'.

When the moderators emerged as a group with their own identity, it shaped the discussion in the forums; it was

> the nerds and the really nerdy geeks. You get people who have really weird senses of humour, who are very – not talking about me – very intelligent, college degrees, PhDs, mathematicians, scientists. If you go into the forum right now, we've got a core selection of probably some of the smartest people in the world.

The tone on the forums is 'being very, very serious in a fun way'.

> It's all about being weird and silly and off the wall and little jokes will run within the forum. You have to be there for a long time to get the reoccurring jokes but that's how families are, families have their own little inside jokes. Silly behaviour is encouraged as long as it's clever.

There are jokes which only people interested in math will get scattered throughout the forum. For instance, the calendar which when clicked, goes to January 2038 (Unix time).

Emoticons are used in all forums but in Mersenne they took a more personal twist. They are customized and named after people so they match their personalities. Vang who makes most of them, says he would see a new one and think, 'hey, this sure reminds me of Bob or this guy or that guy'. In GIMPs, the analogy to a family is made repeatedly by a number of interviewees. Vang says:

> To the point where we had a guy a few years ago, his name was Vallie and at that time he had done the most number of posts. His posts were for the most part weird, he was an old guy, he would confuse his math, he would make suggestions that were kind of sketchy, but it's like you have a family in real life, you have an uncle who's a little off, maybe he's got a speech impediment or one leg. Someone else might want to make fun of him but you'll go to his defence, it's ok for you to make fun of him because you're in the family but if

someone else does, no. So he's not posting one day and that was a shock because he posted a lot and then a few days later, his son comes on to say "hi, my dad was Vallie, and we're just here to say it's all he ever talked about you know...".

Although there is admiration and respect for BOINC on the Mersenne forum, it is seen as too focused on the competition aspect, 'sterile, you have all these little communities with little outposts in the middle of nowhere and not really talking to each other' (Vang). The competitive aspect is still there in GIMPS but it is less immediate and more based on the science and math, the race to discover rather than to win. GIMPs work units take much longer than the average VDC work unit.

The community within the Mersenne forum is international in membership, as are all VDC projects. Seeing the spread of countries that participants come from conveys how truly international VDC activity is; a place where international communication is made possible for many people who would not otherwise have the opportunity to engage with people from other places. For many, this encourages a fresh perspective and understanding of people who come from other cultures. A long time moderator who prefers to remain anonymous described how he

> live[s] in a town [in US] you can't even imagine how desolate and bleak educationally and philosophically it is. Where I live it's "kill all the rag heads" and "forget civil rights" and "God hates homosexuals" and I live in the worst place that a liberal minded person could ever live. I walk around and think to myself am I the only person in this city, who thinks outside of what they were brought up to believe...and the only thing that kept me from being there myself is my involvement in computers and hanging out with other people in the VDC forums.

Going for a forum like Mersenne is the best way for a small group that is aiming for stability and longevity. A GIMPS supermoderator argues there is a choice:

> if your goal is to maximize production, you make a very slick graphical interface, a fancy website, you have really big numbers and celebrities. You know DC is like a binary game, you can play it totally commercial, very slick and a lot of the newer projects are like that. Those communities don't have sub-communities within those communties and the overall large community is never going to become stable with the skills of the sub communities.

Big new projects attract a lot of people initially but it's the ones that invest more in the members and actually build up relationships that last longer, and which the members really care about how others in the forum perceive them, and want to contribute as much as they can, that develop into strong communities of like-minded people.

Chapter 5

Competition and Co-opetition: The Race to Discover and to Win

The competition that the "team" aspect fosters is also interesting. It's like cooperative opposition where society benefits and it's all in good fun (Respondent to survey of VDC, 2010–11).

It's enjoyable for most of the same reasons online gaming is enjoyable. Friendly competition between geographically separated people of similar mindedness... (Respondent to survey of VDC, 2010–11).

Motivation in Teams and Online Forums

Individually manifested altruism in its various forms, an interest in science and a sense of community is not enough to explain why millions participate and why for thousands it becomes a regular and intrinsic part of their lives through participation in teams and online forums. My research indicates that the answer lies in the intersection of motivation and the interactional and organizational possibilities emerging through the Internet. The network organizational form can capture people's motivation better than hierarchical organizations and channel it in a self-sustaining mode (Weber, 2004). Specifically, the Internet based community allows competition and cooperation simultaneously. The Internet allows the formation of virtual teams of participants that cooperate by sharing knowledge and expertise and compete against other such teams.

Through the Internet, both individual and team participants in VDC can be rewarded in ways that encourages further participation. Beenan et al. (2004) state that participants in collective projects will not typically persist in participation, or will participate minimally, if they feel their contribution is not 'special', no matter how important the altruistic elements of the project are to them; they will become 'social loafers'. Beenan et al. begin by observing that people exert less effort on a collective task than they do on a comparable individual task. They posit a collective effort model that identifies conditions under which people will be less inclined to social loafing. These conditions include (a) believing that their effort is important to the group's performance, (b) believing that their contributions to the group are identifiable, and (c) liking the group they are working with.

In VDC, an individual's prominence in terms of the contribution to the project and compared to other participants is rendered visible through project websites where statistical tables of contributions are posted. Participants can also work in teams which come together to compete within a particular project, and in forums where teams discuss strategy and share technical tips to aid their quest to achieve higher rankings in the statistics tables.

In addition, abundant research since the 1960s shows that providing people with specific, high-challenge goals stimulates higher task performance than easy or 'do your best' goals (Locke and Latham, 2002). The design recommendation from the goal-setting literature for online communities is that these communities should set specific and challenging contribution goals for their members, both individuals and teams, and provide statistical information on achievement of those goals by individuals and teams on the project websites (Soares et al., 1998).

Crunching

For many volunteers, some scale of judgement is essential to make VDC challenging. From the beginning in the stand alone projects and then in BOINC, credits have been awarded for each work unit crunched. Each project has a website where the contributions of each individual are recorded and tables rank teams, and within teams, individuals are ranked for their processing contribution. BOINC also has an overall league table where individuals and teams that contribute to several projects compete to see who is contributing the most overall in BOINC. All tables change constantly to reflect the changes in credits being accomplished by the various teams and individuals.

To properly motivate the participants it is critical that an appropriate metric be found to measure the amount of computational effort expended by each participant. As one of the forum members pointed out in survey, this metric must be

> ...fair, accurate, and cheater-proof...This metric is more or less cast in stone, because zeroing out the scoreboard and starting over will cause many participants to quit the project. The metric must take care to motivate the right participant behavior and not create a conflict of interest between the project leadership and the volunteer participants, because most project participants are caught up in the competitive aspect and if there is a conflict between goals of the project (scientific benefits) and maximizing their own score, many participants will choose the latter.

This metric is usually expressed in terms of the number of Work Units completed. However in the case when tasks vary in size, this is not sufficient and the metric is usually the amount of computational time expended. If the correlation between the credit awarded and the actual time spent completing a task is not precise, it gives the participants that are caught up in the competitive aspect of the project an incentive to only do tasks that require proportionately less time for the credit awarded. While this is not necessarily cheating it does create an incentive that is not in the interest of the project. On the other hand, this mechanism may be exploited by the project managers to give priority to a work category within the project if required. For example, in the GIMPS project, in order to encourage more participants to do a type of processing known as 'Lucas-Lehmer testing' as opposed to another type known as 'factoring', the latter is disincentivized by awarding 30 per cent less credit for the same amount of computing time spent on both work types. This helps keep the right balance of participants performing both work types as 'factoring' requires only about 10 per cent as much work as 'Lucas-Lehmer testing' does.

It is essential that the credit system works effectively and this is the responsibility of the individual project scientists and programmers. The overall credit framework for the projects participating through BOINC is the responsibility of David Anderson and his team at University of California, Berkeley. Anderson says: 'I personally put a lot of energy into setting up mechanisms that make such competition possible'. For BOINC, the essential requirement is providing a way to add up the points for participants contributing to multiple projects. All the projects have their own databases, teams and users so Anderson devised a way of associating the accounts on the different projects through email addresses. They also of course have to be kept private. 'I create the machinery that makes these different competition schemes possible. And then I leave it to other people to implement them and develop websites where teams can challenge each other and stuff like that'.

Teams

So why, if there are millions of potential participants in a VDC project and the number of people involved in teams is – as we show later – nowhere near that, are teams important?

There is no centralized authority directing how the projects should be run and the practice of millions of people simultaneously doing the same thing, downloading data and processing it without any central instruction. The use of teams to drive the production of work units – using cooperation on the team to drive competition that contributes to the larger cooperative task of producing work units – is a very successful strategy used in Voluntary Distributed Computing.

The answer also lies, as Weber (2004) noted with regard to Open-Source Software (OSS) projects, in the fact that even if the number of participants is very big, it says nothing about the scope of contributions. In OSS, only a subset of users contribute in significant ways. In a case study of the Open-Source Apache server, Mockus et al. (2000) showed that 85–90 per cent of the code was written by about 15 developers. A greater number helped fix defects and a greater number again helped report problems. In a survey of 100 OSS projects by Krishnamurthy (2002) it was found that the majority of mature OSS projects were carried out by a very small number of developers, most commonly one person. Healy and Schussman (2003) argue from this that participation is skewed both within projects and between projects, with a small number of people doing the hard-core programming and a small number of projects attracting most activity. In VDC too, the contribution of a small proportion of participants in VDC accounts for a disproportionately large amount of results and has a disproportionately large impact on the rest of the VDC community.

In general, a relatively small percentage of participants are part of a team in any given Voluntary Distributed Computing project. However, participants that are part of a team are usually more 'productive' and more enthusiastic about the project. This is particularly true of teams that organize around forums and is evidenced by their success in terms of their contribution to the projects themselves. The proportional contribution from participants who are members of a team varies a lot from project to project as some are more conducive to team formation whereas others are not so conducive. It also depends on the history of the project and the stage at which it was adopted by the major teams in Distributed Computing. In GIMPS, for instance, as of February 2005, Holohan and Garg (2005) reported that the top two teams contributed over 10 per cent of the total project output and the top 10 teams over 18 per cent. In SETI@home, which is a much larger project, the top 10 teams still combined to produce 7.6 per cent of the work. This was a significant amount as the combined 50,000 or so participants that are part of these 10 teams make up less than 1 per cent of the over 5 million participants in SETI and yet have done 7.6 per cent of the work in the project.

Thus, teams are important because they reward participation and as we shall also show, are particularly important for people who are the most productive participants.

The volunteers on mersenneforum.org on the other hand, are affiliated to the project and not always part of a team.

SETI@home incorporated team formation from the beginning and they allowed teams to be formed in the following categories – schools and colleges, companies, clubs and government agencies. The first two categories were further subdivided into primary and secondary schools, junior colleges, universities and departments and into small, medium and large companies. Of these, clubs are perhaps the only group that relies on self-organization and thus uses forums as an online meeting point for the members since the members of 'club' teams usually do not have any meeting place in real life. It is an example of the strength of the collaborative process that all of the top 10 teams in the SETI team contribution statistics are club teams as of late 2012.

A key difference between Open Source Software and Voluntary Distributed Computing is the competitive element in VDC, including the formation of teams that compare with each other in league tables. The communitarian ethos of OSS is there but contains an element of competition within the overall framework of contribution to a communitarian goal.

Altruistic Game-Playing

It all sounds a lot like a game and arguably one way to describe the competition through cooperation in VDC is altruistic game-playing. The outcome benefits humankind and that benefit increases the more you compete against other individuals and teams as that means more data produced. Although gaming is seen as increasingly central to almost every field of endeavour in the networked information economy (Chatfield, 2010), and hence gaining respectability, this has not been the case in the industrial economy. Games are an intrinsic part of childhoods around the world, and apart from fun, help a child learn and be socialized into their community and culture. However, game playing among adults (apart from sport) has had negative connotations and been marginalized in industrial societies. Anthropologist Richard Schechner (1988) has noted, 'In the West, [adult] play is a rotten category tainted by unreality, inauthenticity, duplicity, make-believe, looseness, fooling around, and inconsequentiality'.

Childhood games are as often as not multiplayer and such multiplayer games are ubiquitous in human cultures around the world and often have important social functions such as acquisition of social and political skills, conflict resolution and role appropriate behaviour (Schechner and Schuman 1976; Turner 1982; Sutton-Smith 1981). It was an aberration that computer games, in the early days, were individual games. But the rise of networks changed that, and from the moment networks began to appear in labs on college campuses, people tried to play on them with other people.

Much of today's online gaming challenges the negative perception, placing an increasing emphasis on cooperation and collective behaviour between players (Nardi and Harris, 2000). In Massively Multiplayer Online Games (MMOG), such as World of Warcraft, and Massively Multiplayer Online Roleplaying Games (MMORPG), such as Second Life, collective behaviour occurs all the time. In MMOGs, the design of the game itself makes cooperation between players a necessity. The more and better quality of cooperation, the more the player wins. These online social games, similarly to VDC, provide a field in which the drive to play games and compete is combined with an empathic drive for altruistic behaviour, providing a significant opportunity to see an evolution in human collective behaviour (Pearce, 2010).

Characters in MMOGs are from different systems with different strengths and weaknesses. Consequently, cooperation is required to progress as a player may need to accomplish a task for which he or she does not have the skills (Nardi and

Harris, 2006). Because of this many groups are formed within the game. These groups are often defined by a shared goals, shared identities, or shared real world affiliations (religious, geographical, etc). Researchers have noted a high degree of solidarity in these groups (known as guilds). Guild members will look out for one another both in gameplay and in real life, sometimes staging interventions if they feel a guild member has been online too much.

In VDC, the use of teams to drive the production of work units – using cooperation on the team to drive competition that contributes to the larger cooperative task of producing work units – is the most successful strategy used so far in Voluntary Distributed Computing to drive up contributions. Participants are cooperating together on a particular project towards the goal of scientific research most broadly and on the specific scientific goals of the project, e.g. finding life in outer space in SETI. If they are a member of a team, they are simultaneously competing with the other teams in the project on the more immediate goal of racking up the most contributions and coming out on top of the table of statistics documenting contributions, producing a form of cooperation and competition, the so-called 'co-opetition' or in the words of the survey participant quoted at the start of the chapter, 'cooperative opposition'.

Teams have been part of Voluntary Distributed Computing since the beginning. A team typically consists of a group of people with a common affiliation such as the same school, university or place of work, that pool their contributions to compete against other teams. However, a shared affiliation is not necessary and some of the most successful teams have been those that have formed out of a common interest such as 'Team Art Bell' in SETI that was formed out of the listeners of Art Bell's late night radio show or 'The Knights Who Say Ni!' formed by a group of Monty Python fans.

The level of interaction amongst team members varies widely and typically teams formed due to a common interest of the members have greater interaction. The latter are made of 'active' participants that identify themselves with the group they are part of as opposed to teams formed due to some institutional affiliation where membership is a passive activity and does not require exercise of free choice. The size of a team also varies widely from teams consisting of only one member to teams such as Team Art Bell and SETI.Germany with over 10,000 participants each.

Proportionately they are big contributors with over 10 per cent of credits awarded to just 0.2 per cent of volunteers. They enjoy the prestige, which is what keeps them at it and they make posts in forums when they reach milestones, for which they receive praise. They also often display their credit scores in their forum signature and it is seen as a genuine accomplishment. The activity of volunteer online forums is crucial because there are so many volunteers reading and posting on them that this reassures the Super-Crunchers that it is worthwhile to post about achieving credit milestones because these posts will be noticed by many others.

Peer recognition derives from the desire for fame and esteem, which is also associated with future returns. Feedback always has a positive effect in that it shows volunteers that their contributions mean something. Thus the feedback mechanism is self-reinforcing, for it encourages the author to expend additional effort to perfect his code, which in turn attracts more favourable feedback.

Daruch and Carusi (2010) conclude that a good credit system and visibility of results and accomplishments is crucial to recruiting and retaining volunteers. They recommend a credit system that is easy to understand, reliable, transparent, cumulative, comparative, updated regularly and most critically, a system that is visible and where volunteers are publicly hailed when they achieve milestones. In short, to emphasize the game aspects with rules, fairness and winning to the fore. Einstein@home has paid particular attention to this and it has paid off in consistently high volunteer attention – and hence contributions – to the project.

In online social gaming also, random acts of help or kindness occur on a regular basis, with players aiding other players by protecting them in battle (a practice known as 'buffing'), or helping them to complete tasks. In this way the game design can be seen to promote a rather utopic form of collective behaviour, based on cooperation rather than competition.

But we need to stop and ask, are we stretching things too far in deeming VDC to be a form of 'gaming'? It is useful to consider the literature on play and games and to see if VDC satisfies the criteria for a 'game'.

Johan Huizinga, considered the father of 'ludology' (a term used to describe the study of digital games), defines play as

> a free activity standing quite consciously outside "ordinary" life as being "not serious", but at the same time absorbing the player intensely and utterly. It is an activity connected with no material interest, and no profit can be gained by it. It proceeds within its own proper boundaries of time and space according to fixed rules in an orderly manner. It promotes the formation of social groupings which tend to surround themselves with secrecy and to stress their difference from the common world by disguise or other means (1950[1938]: 13).

There are numerous and conflicting definitions of a 'game' (Zimmerman, 2004: 71–84) but most game researchers would agree that a game is a formal system for structured play constrained by a set of rules that prescribe the means of achieving a specified goal (Suits 1967; 1978; DeKoven 1978; Pearce 1997; Salen and Zimmerman 2004; Fullerton, Swain and Hoffman 2004; Juul 2005).

Although there are definite goals, in VDC, as in the MMOG where it is a subscription based ongoing world of play, it is not appropriate to consider 'winning' or 'losing' as the ongoing nature of DC and daily updates preclude the closure typically associated with traditional games.

A useful way of thinking about VDC in gaming terms is through the ideas of 'ludic' versus 'paidiac' worlds. In a key work by Caillois (1961: 13), games are characterized as 'ludus' and open-ended creative, non goal based or 'sandbox' type play as 'paidiac' although these two play forms exist on a spectrum and can share a number of qualities in common. As the primary distinction between these concepts is that ludic worlds present the player with a prescribed overarching goal while paidiac worlds do not, it would seem that VDC is 'ludic'. However, the project and team websites and forums, with areas designated as 'lounges', 'cafe's', 'puzzles', and other general terms for an adult 'sandbox' would have a strong claim to be 'paidiac' worlds.

All virtual worlds, whether ludic or paidiac, have rules, that Pearce (2010: 29) calls '[virtual] world rules', which provide limits and shape the behaviour in online gaming scenarios such as VDC. These include communication protocols and their effects. Forums is clearly the preferred mode for those involved in VDC. BOINC has recently introduced the option of 'skype' advice sessions which despite adding 'bandwidth', i.e. synchronous, visual and aural communication, have had a very low take-up rate. Anderson explained:

> So we set up this other way of doing customer support but based on skype. Which I think is a great idea but it hasn't really achieved the level of users I would like. Skype has the ability to query a particular user and see if they are online – you can't see that from a programme. We have a system where people can sign up to be customer support volunteers and they tell us their skype id and they tell us what languages that they speak. And then there's a web page that people can go to, to get technical help where they click on the language that they speak and they see a bunch of volunteers that are available to provide help in that language. They can see which of them are currently online with skype and they can call them on skype. The idea is that when you have a conversation with somebody like a live back and forth conversation you can very quickly figure out what terminology they use what words they understand or don't understand. A simple problem, you know a typical problem can usually be diagnosed in about ten seconds. But it's not being used, we're having in the order you know of 20 or 50 calls per day, whereas there would be thousands of messages looking for help coming in on the boards.

Several interviewees stated that they like the asynchronous nature of the message boards or forums as they allowed time to think, and do research on a problem, before replying. Emotionally, several moderators said it is useful because it slows down response times and people have time to reflect or sleep on it before replying if an emotionally challenging post is made. Emotions do run high whether it is to do with individuals caught cheating (as in the individual on an ArsTechnica team who admitted cheating to his team-mates), or sexist or anti-tech, or impatient replies which are in themselves potentially upsetting, or responses which can escalate a situation (as in the case on the Mersenne Forum where one moderator who later had to be banned was constantly insulting people for not being as knowledgeable as himself).

VDC has explicit rules analogous to 'the core formal system that constitutes how a game functions' and therefore are distinguishable from diverse strategies that individual players may use to play the game (Salen and Zimmerman, 2004: 121).

Rules limit players' actions, are explicit and unambiguous, are shared by all players, and are fixed, binding, and repeatable over time and by multiple players (Salen and Zimmerman, 2004). By these criteria, VDC has indeed strong elements of 'gaming' in its rules, roles and dynamics.

There is sometimes tension between VDC crunchers with a logic of expediency and players with more reflectively moral-political logic. Some volunteers pointedly say that they are not in it for the credits but for the science, dismissing those who are relentless in their pursuit of credits. But of course games that encourage expediency are not inherently unethical nor unproductive. Expediency stems from the same Latin root as 'expedite' and shares its meaning of forwarding matters swiftly, being helpful or serviceable (Raphael et al., 2010). Gamers participate in VDC effectively and can be non-reflexively altruistic while doing so.

Enlightened Self-Interest

Why does it matter if VDC fits the criteria for a game? The answer is it does not theoretically, but it does in practical terms. The competition element is key to recruiting and retaining people. Many people who compete do so in teams and those that utilize forums to strategize and communicate with team members forge strong bonds which promote commitment to the respective project or team. Thus, forums help competition and at the same time they foster civic life which reinforces the bonds that helps the participants compete successfully to increase their credits and contribute to their project of choice. Getting people together who are not otherwise connected to each other not only reduces any sense of isolation (which I show below increases efficacy), but also offers the potential for meaningful interaction and political activity. In the eighteenth century Alexis de Tocqueville argued that self-interest (participating in a project that means something to us, or achieving as many credits as possible) and interpersonal unity (belonging to a project where other people are also pursuing the project's scientific goals, or belonging on a team) are reconcilable when we recognize shared interests, i.e. develop 'enlightened self-interest'. People learn to link their own desires to those of other isolated citizens by being part of associations; in VDC's case, projects, teams and forums. For instance, in a democracy, one cannot simply want lower taxes and expect the government to respond. One must find others who have similar wishes and to experience the personal desire for lower taxes as a goal larger than any single person (Schulze, 2011). This enlightened self-interest is what DeTocqueville calls 'self-interest rightly understood' (2007: 463).

This connection of self to society is reflected in the comments from participants in a wide range of projects.

Linking one's own interest with the broader good is particularly common among the volunteers on medical science related projects. A sample from the second survey supports this:

Table 5.1   Enlightened self-interest: Community related motivations of participants in survey of volunteers 2010–11

I'm getting older each day and the sooner those old age diseases are eradicated the better.
I feel I am making a useful contribution to society.
The only contribution I can do for mankind. I feel part of something huge.
It's a simple way to benefit everyone altruistically.
The research supported by Folding@home (my VDC of preference) may one day help my neighbours, my family, or even me. If I can help make that difference, then I want to. I make it a secondary goal to inform others of this project and hopefully inspire them to contribute also. The more donors we have, the faster research is propelled forward, which in turn can help reduce suffering from these diseases.
It can bring humanity a step forward.
It's the community that gives you a great feeling. Just to be part of it. No matter what you contribute. It's even great to help people online with VDC or personal problems.
It is a use of technology where I feel I can personally contribute to the greater good, i.e. curing diseases.
We have idle resources laying around and big mathematical, scientific, health, etc questions to solve...why not work on them!
I'd like to think that I was indirectly involved in research that could help all mankind cure or avoid some horrible diseases.
Mostly a notion of "worthiness" which is hard to define. Basically, if I thought it was making a reasonable advance, it was worthwhile. Still, I also did projects like SETI whose "advance" was a bit of a long shot. But, it looked to me like a good long shot.
I am making a positive contribution to society.
I like the idea of helping to do research with the unused cycles of my computers. Combine that with millions around the world, and there are numerous ideas to explore and understand. I want to help be a part of this.

My primary project is the fight AIDS@home one, chosen because my brother died of AIDS, and I feel like I'm doing something that might prevent others from having to go through the same horrible experience. My mother recently died of Alzheimer's, and as Alzheimer's VDC projects become available, I will contribute to those as well.

Folding@home because they research diseases that affected my grandparents and I want a cure before it affects me.

Hopes of finding cures for cancer.

Traditional group life achieves through associations' decisions on group goals that each individual has an incentive to promote. The noble result of doing disease research can come out of the desire for advancing science, and personal victory and approbation from one's peers when multiple people with the same desires cooperate. What matters is not the content of the group interest but the *mechanism* of uniting individual wishes into a common interest. VDCs, like video games, are excellent tools for realizing 'enlightened self interest' because they unite players, in spite of any differences the players may have, and reward those who are able to work toward a common end. Each player must learn not only to be part of a team but also to subordinate personal concerns to those of the group and to tie their own desires to the group's goals, i.e. they encourage team work. Teams obviously fare much better when players cooperate, helping other players helps oneself as a constituent part of the team.

When there are real people to witness one's actions, the actions take on new meaning. People are able to show respect and give praise in a way that computer programs cannot (Beberg, 2009). Being part of a team encourages continued participation because it promotes feelings of efficacy, giving team-members a sense of accomplishment. Individuals tend to underestimate what they can accomplish (like feeling their vote does not matter in large democracies). Participation in groups and teams is at a size in which volunteers can meaningfully participate, getting confidence through seeing the results of their actions at a local level. It overcomes feelings of insignificance that can come from being part of a very large project. Confidence comes from performing well in competition with other people and through mastery of the technological aspects of VDC as it usually involves learning, including new skills. There are constantly new challenges to speed up computers and solve problems; improvement gives participants the feeling of accomplishment, promoting self-esteem and self-efficacy (Lieberman, 2006).

Mike, a long-time volunteer, recalls how he started crunching for Ubero, a what he calls 'fun' VDC project which was using DC to map the Internet. Ubero had a timer inside the programme that limited the rate at which the volunteer could complete workunits. An instance (work unit) would start, stop after 10 seconds and then the programme would pause for 5 minutes. Mike found a way to start an instance, stop it after the 10 second completion point and then start a new instance, keeping the program running continuously. He went to the top of the charts as his work unit completion rate accelerated very fast. He recalls:

> within a matter of weeks I was at the top of the chart on Ubero. There were thousands and thousands of people and they were probably thinking "wow what is this guy doing here". And I published the trick on the forum, I gave them the whole trick how to do it and then it was just neat for a day or a week or whatever it was to be the top guy, taking advantage of and exploiting the system.

At the volunteer level, VDC projects, are, in theory like the democratic societies studied and theorized by DeTocqueville, meritocratic and democratic: each participant is equal and achieved status is the only legitimate basis on which to rank individuals in the league tables of the projects. Players' race, gender and beliefs do not matter – participants judge each other on skill and commitment more than anything else. Those who contribute the most stand out because of their ability and commitment rather than any status they have in the real world.

In practice, VDC, like online games are not always egalitarian and fair. Nardi and Harris (2006) note how some players will prey on weakened players after fights to gain their possessions. It is precisely because the ranks are a mark of hard work that the most serious accusation that can be made is that a participant is cheating. The most common form of cheating is volunteers installing clients on machines they do not own at school or work in an effort to increase their personal or team statistics. More damaging is the use of Trojan horses on P2P file sharing systems to install the client and gain in the statistics. Both are easily noticed by system administrators and by other participants noticing rapidly rising users and teams (Beberg et al., 2009). Just as other participants are able to show respect and give praise in a way that computer programs cannot, they can also judge each other and reinforce rules that make cheating far more difficult. Other participants watch carefully for violation of the meritocratic gaming norms and censure anyone who violates them. Typically censure means that users' statistics are zeroed and they are blacklisted.

Many volunteers and professionals involved in VDC noted that the competitive element satisfied the competitive 'instinct' (Tony, a volunteer) people had. David Anderson of BOINC commented: 'People, and especially men are competitive animals and I view it as an updated version for men who like to buy cars with big powerful engines back in the 60s and 70s. The idea of hotrodding and they would race each other and so forth. Now they're running very fast computers, a lot of them overclock [deliberately change the hardware to work faster] their computers to race against each other'.

One project, the Seventeen or Bust (SoB) Project, illustrates the strength of co-opetition in a collaborative context. This project aims to prove the Sierpinski conjecture by finding a prime number of the form $k*2^n+1$ for every k less than 78557. Since a number can be proven not prime but breaking it into its constituent factors, a sub-project of Seventeen or Bust tries to eliminate possible candidates quickly by a process called sieving.

The initial sieve client was very slow. However, over the course of one and a half years in 2003–2004 and through the collaboration of three programmers the sieving program is now about 100 times as fast as the original. What is interesting is that this impromptu collaboration occurred through the SoB project forum online and the participants came from different countries, did not know each other, and had not worked together before. They all participated in the discussion in the Sieve Client Thread <http://www.free-dc.org/forum/showthread.php?s=andthreadid=2408> which received a total of 716 posts! The collaboration was not limited to the three people who did the actual programming, but several other participants in the discussion who suggested ideas, tested initial versions of the program and found bugs, gave encouragement to and motivated the programmers who were, it must be remembered, working for free. This was also a limited example of Open-Source Software within VDC as the source code for the sieve client program was shared amongst the programmers.

The initial thrust came from competition between two participants 'FatPhil' and 'paul.jobling' who competed with each other to improve their own versions of the client and make it faster than the other. Eventually one of them dropped out and provided his source code to the other who integrated the techniques of both programs to provide a program which was faster still. Eventually a third person took over the project.

Not everyone of course is driven by competition and the central role of competition ignites some significant tension among volunteers who are not interested in the credits but only in the science. ClimatePrediction.net is a project that has a high number of non-competitive crunchers, partly because CPDN 'does not give very generous credits compared to the other projects', says Maureen, a moderator on CPDN.

> We have kept our credits the same as when we started, virtually no credit inflation, 5 maybe 10 per cent. Other projects have been involved in quite a lot of credit inflation, the projects are run independently, their admin, their scientists can do whatever they want, but of course the figures are all published, the league tables for all the projects on BOINC. If you look at the people and teams that are in the top 100 in the league tables, they are all running the same batch of projects. The reason they're running them is that these particular projects give the most generous credits…if an existing project changes their credits, increases them, and you look at the league table, it will reflect that.

She went on to say that there was a lot of resistance among volunteers in CPDN to the proposal of increasing credits as they felt it would lose them people who are in it for the science.

In practice, there is a dividing line between people who are more ideologically committed, who choose their projects carefully, and the 'gamers', who are interested primarily in credits and winning. Both kinds of volunteers co-exist in the same project, sometimes in the same person! Several volunteers spoke of how they began by being driven only by the credits but over time became more interested in one or two projects and devoted their resources to those with the competition factor becoming secondary. Ideologically driven participants are likely to be driven to be just as productive as the crunchers driven by credit competition, as was found in a study of Open-Source developers where ideological commitment was a significant promoter of team output and retention of participants (Stewart and Gosain, 2006).

In sum, the individuals involved in VDC can maximize their power, both in terms of achieving scientific goals and personal competitive goals, through cooperation. VDC projects bring individuals together in an environment that encourages competition and cooperation to overcome challenges.

Case Study: ArsTechnica (www.arstechnica.com)

The ArsTechnica forum is one of three long-running technical websites, not originating in VDC, which do news reporting on technology related stories and also have forums. Most of these forums are to discuss technology, not necessarily related to VDC – for instance, different operating systems and hardware issues. But they also have forums which are dedicated to all things distributed computing.

Between 1995 and 2001, when SETI@home was the 'only show in town' as volunteer AG put it, a team on ArsTechnica joined the SETI@home project and called itself Team Lamb Chop, eventually attracting 500 members at its peak. Other teams in the other broad technology sites forums had an official policy of only promoting one project and they would not crunch for any other project or form a team on any other project. The ArsTechnica forum and Team Lamb Chop had a more inclusive philosophy; any participant in the forum or on the team could promote another project and recruit members to that project.

AG began crunching for SETI@home as part of the UCLA SETI team where he was a graduate student, but once he discovered ArsTechnica, he left the UCLA team for Team Lamb Chop and subsequently discovered and joined more projects. Due to the inclusive philosophy, AG was offered other projects, and other participants would suggest they get a team together on ArsTechnica. The person who brought the team to the attention of the community had naming rights and was known as the founder of the team. Each person though would have to divide their existing resources at home (CPU capacity) between the teams they were members of. In 2001–2003, this was not a problem as there were four main projects which people in ArsTechnica crunched for: SETI@ home, Folding@home, Distributed.Net, and GIMPs. By 2004, there were up to 50 projects vying for the attention of the teams and friction began to emerge as volunteer resources were spread more thinly. It became chaotic and people started to choose one home project and stick with that. This prompted Mike, a member of Team Lamb Chop to propose a new team specializing in crunching for GIMPS. As founder, he called it Team Prime Rib, and several members of the ArsTechnica subsequently moved with him when he moved the team's home to the Mersenne Forum, dedicated primarily to GIMPS.

At the peak of ArsTechnica, in the early 2000s, the main motivation in the forum was to keep each team high in the different project's rankings. The forum developed a 'flying squad', which was a bunch of mobile volunteers, in the sense that they did not have any project affiliation and could move from project to project. If an ArsTechnica team was doing badly on a particular project or was in danger of being overtaken by another team in the rankings, the flying squad would swoop in and volunteer for a week or weeks to increase the ranking of the team in that particular project. The people 'didn't care about the the project they were donating their computer power to; they only cared about the ranking of the ArsTechnica team in that particular project'. (AG) AFS activity was usually accompanied by a flurry of activity on the online forum as well as in the IRC chat rooms as decisions were made and members mobilized in completely decentralized fashion in a non-hierarchical structure.

> Crunchers who did have project affiliations developed less radical mobile tactics. Some projects would do particularly well on particular computers, so "for example, intel computers were very good on certain projects and AMD computers were better at certain other projects. So people did swop computers, if I liked an Intel loving project and I had an AMD computer, I would swop my computer with someone I knew whose preferences were, whose situation was reversed" (Paul).

The high point in competition was the ArsTechnica team SETI holding the number one team position in the SETI rankings for a year ('causing much jubilation' recalls AG) from 2001. Then the team was over taken in the rankings by another team from outside ArsTechnica and it became clear that despite all the resources the ArsTechnica volunteer community threw at the task, it was impossible to beat the new comer, which had many more volunteers than ArsTechnica. It also had some 'heavy hitters' – people who had at their disposal maybe 100 computers in a company or university, who would bring the entire computing power of that company or university to the disposal of the team.

AG says

> Competition played a huge part. Most people – including me at the time – were motivated by seeing their name at the top of the list or seeing the name of their team at the top of the list. That was definitely a huge thing. I'd say the majority of volunteers didn't really care very much about the science behind the projects or any real contributions they would have. They had computers, it was like a game for them, instead of playing a video game they were basically making the computer process things in the background and seeing the stats rack up.

A number of playful projects came up as a result of this. One project counted how much the volunteer moved their mouse, racking up the meters or kilometres that the mouse moved in months or days or weeks. A similar project called Pulse counted the number of times that the volunteer tapped their keyboard.

Cheating became a serious problem, 'as less scrupulous participants decided that they wanted to gain in the statistics and get to the top using ways other than the fairest of ways' (Mike). One such perpetrator came from inside the ArsTechnica SETI@home team at the end of 2000. The founders of SETI were aware of the problem of cheating and to stamp it out, required every work unit to be processed by at least 2 sometimes 3 people and they only accepted results that matched the other results. But the perpetrator in the ArsTechnica team found a way to send the results in without actually doing any processing and in doing so, was able to artificially inflate his figures, and became the leading cruncher on the ArsTechnica SETI team. He was 'lionized' by the other members until he himself confessed to what he had been doing, and did so in a way that was dismissive of the other members of the team who had been treating him with such respect as a supercruncher. There was a lot of anger and he was told to pack his technical bags and leave the team and forum.

Competition bred innovation. ArsTechnica increased the competitive spirit through their presentation of statistics in two ways. First, the statistics on SETI@home's project website were updated on an hourly basis and the ArsTechnica SETI team had its own statistics website as well which pulled down the results from the SETI servers and then displayed all the rankings. The SETI website did not keep a historical record of contributions but ArsTechnica kept a database of rankings so on any day a cruncher was able to see their average production rate and where their rank was projected to be 7 days, or 30 days or 90 days in the future. Crunchers wanted to be able to see graphs of their contributions and 'to be able to get a sense of who the threats were' (AG), i.e. who the people were behind them in the ranks, who was out producing them, and who were the targets, the people who were ahead of them in the ranks so they could plan and project overtaking dates.

> It was a game. You certainly got a great rush at winning or doing better at the game than you did before. For example, if you were able to find an extra computer somewhere in your office or get a friend to run the client on their computer, that would basically increase your production and help you move up the rankings. There were people who spent a fair bit of time and money buying in computers with the express purposes of crunching work for the projects and rising in the ranks (AG).

On the SETI@home website, the teams rankings were listed and within the ArsTechnica forum, all the individual contributors to the team were listed and ranked.

Competition also bred useful skills for social action. In ArsTechnica, volunteers were allowed to recruit other volunteers from existing projects, but in a climate where quite a few people were annoyed at people coming up with new projects and drawing away computing resources from existing ones. Recruitment was a delicate business, there was a certain political element there. You had to attract members to the new project, without kind of ruffling feathers and do it in a way that made the project sound quite exciting. Of course, there was a certain percentage of people who would try any new project just for the novelty, but to have people stay crunching in a project and for that team to become an important team within the ArsTechnica community required you know certain ingenuity and a certain amount of skill and political skills (AG).

Chapter 6
Moderators, Super-Moderators, Beta Testers and Translators

It turns out that [some] volunteers do all sorts of work other than just volunteering computing power. You definitely need to figure out how to use those people (David Anderson of BOINC).

Although all nodes in a network are connected and thus in theory a network is egalitarian to a degree impossible in hierarchical organizations or collectivities, in fact all nodes are not equal. All networks have similar patterns – they are bunched around hubs into which the majority of links go (Barabasi, 2003). Granovetter (1973) recognized this in his emphasis on the importance of bridges – those nodes that link clusters to other clusters.

VDC is a combination of network and hierarchy. The scientists are at the top of the pyramid, then the system administrators, then the super-volunteers (the super-moderators and the moderators) and the mass of volunteers at the base.

In VDC, BOINC is obviously the centre of the network, the hub into which most projects link, although some like GIMPS do not link in. GIMPS is however connected through the individuals who are active on the GIMPS project but also active on projects through the BOINC framework. The projects themselves are hubs of their own network with all participants linking in to the homepage, and many into the forums and team home pages. Within a project's network, some links or nodes or volunteers are more connected than others – they are the moderators or supervolunteers who include those who do more than download and run the programme, and participate in the forums. They take on additional roles and jobs, most commonly as moderators on the forum but also as beta testers of new versions of project software, and translators of webpages and forum content into language other than the home language of the project. There are also the moderators of the moderators, called supermoderators or 'supermods'.

Moderators in particular are a relatively invisible, definitely unheralded, yet crucial part of VDC infrastructure and community life. Without them, VDC would not be possible. A great deal of time needs to be spent helping people getting software applications, called clients, running and responding to questions. Most often those in need of help are new volunteers, who are unfamiliar with how to run the clients or find answers to their questions. Charles, a moderator on ClimatePrediction.net (CPDN) describes how:

One basic function is customer support. When a new volunteer comes along, quite likely a non-technical person who doesn't understand anything about computers and they experience some sort of glitch in getting the software to work and you know usually it's just that they weren't following instructions. Then you need to have some place to go to get questions answered.

Moderators and volunteers also write third party software add-ons, debug problems, answer new user questions, and do a great deal to promote the project. Any new information tends to propagate through the team sites and forums very quickly, which makes the information even more widely accessible.

There is no way that the Principal Investigator and the usual small scientific team (they usually can be counted on one or two hands), and the paid system administrator, if there is one, can respond (Beberg et al., 2009). Moderators deal with most enquiries themselves but also recognize ones that need to be sent on to the scientific or computer administration people. Dave Anderson of BOINC, says: 'They provide us with a system of triage of these high volume channel message boards'. As one moderator described it,

> Occasionally you do have some questions which you think, oh, actually this is pretty important, that the moderators can bring to the attention of the scientists running the project. There is a role there for the moderators that is sort of allowing scientists to get on with things rather than answering millions of questions.

The second unheralded but critical group are the system administrators. They are usually distinct from the scientific team and are typically career computer personnel, often with an ideological commitment to VDC. As Christian, a system administrator with CPDN, said: 'I put in Silicon Valley hours for academic sector pay'. The key issues for them are the often constant struggle to involve the scientists, and the occasional corruption of behaviour among the moderators. System administrators are part of the lead team of the project but are more constantly involved on a daily basis with moderators and volunteers, particularly the former. They work closely together and share their frustrations and challenges.

A key difference of course is that they are paid employees of the project but their hearts more often than not lie with the moderators and volunteers, the people who are grappling with the everyday computational aspects of VDC and with whom they work much more closely than the scientists. They essentially share the same goals as the volunteers in terms of the substance of their daily activities – getting the hardware and software working, troubleshooting, looking for ways to improve the project. They, as much as the scientist, have a big impact on the moderators' experiences. For the most part, they are very responsive, typically more so than the scientific leads, and have a direct influence in activity on the forums.

System administrators are between the scientific team and the volunteers, and deal mostly with the moderators and super-moderators. As Amy Bruckman (2006) states, 'Culture and technology co-evolve [and] computer professionals catalyze this process'.

Moderators

The tasks of a moderator, broadly defined, are customer support, answering all the queries from volunteers, giving feedback to volunteers, communication of news on the project, liaising between the top of the project, the scientists, and the mass of volunteers, communicating up and down the pyramid. They prevent antisocial or offensive postings or behaviour and where interpersonal issues arise and they do conflict mediation. They can do this because they have the authority to control postings and postings visibility. They can remove offensive or inappropriate posts, give warnings to persistent offenders, and eventually get a person who will not stop offending banned from the site. This is a rare occurrence, but has happened at least once in most projects.

Chris Walsall, a moderator on GIMPS, defines a moderator as:

> Human or humans who are responsible for maintaining the integrity of the forum. The ones who have the responsibility of enforcing the policy of the forum, ensuring that inappropriate content is not posted, that people are not abusive to others, ensuring that everyone plays nice.

Most posters are reasonable but some projects attract more than the usual number of extremists who are not interested in the project so much as propagating particular views. This is exacerbated by the substance of the SETI@home project, the search for extra-terrestrial intelligence. Anderson at BOINC, states:

> All these projects have an area of their message boards where it's supposed to be scientific discussion. And there's a general phenomenon on the internet that people try to vandalize message boards. For example, in the beginning, we were getting religious arguments on a forum that was supposed to be discussing science, trying to goad people into counter attack.

CPDN has experienced similar 'trolling' behaviour around the topic of climate change.

Mike Vang, the founder of the Mersenne Forum who is responsible for the software and server that it sits on, sees the moderators' role as including the approval of posts by new users, as the three first postings of any new user of the forum will be read by a moderator. He says: 'I would argue that at least on Mersenne no level of expertise is required [to be a moderator] beyond not abusing their level of responsibility and enforcing ad hoc rules of the forum'.

Charles, a moderator on CPDN, says what is needed is: 'somebody fairly level headed and posting a lot. They're the two main things I can think of really'.

There is no formal organization of time 'on duty' by the moderators. Like Chris in GIMPS, most moderators would check at least once a day. 'I don't know how many supermods there are, people flow through frequently enough that any issues that need taking care of tend to be taken care of by whoever is on line at that time'.

Beyond these general tasks and orientation, most projects evidence a division of labour within the moderators, sometimes consciously engineered but often produced by people self-selecting for particular types of role and others recognizing their particular expertise and directing inquiries to them for that purpose.

In information communities one often notices that their success depends on individuals playing specific roles. One will be a 'referrer', pointing people to information posted in other sources, or to recent news. Another will be a 'communicator' able to translate in accessible terms complex scientific or technical documents. Another will be a 'problem solver', assisting others in overcoming some difficulty. Another will be a 'moderator', intervening to try to overcome conflict, to bring debate to a higher level of mutual understanding of what is at stake in diverging views. Yet another will be a 'challenger' (of arguments, of explanations). These roles may or may not be formalized in the community processes (in present information communities, it is mostly the notation and moderation – in the sense of control on posting and its visibility – that are made explicit). Of course, most users/contributors will flexibly move from one activity to another: maybe pure consumers of information at most times, at other times answering a question because they happen to know the answer from past experience, occasionally triggered by some contribution to elaborate a much more complex arguement, etc.

The system administration person on CPDN, Carl Christensen, consciously nurtured a team of moderators that could meet the diverse needs of volunteers. Maureen is an untypical volunteer in that she is female and older and not from a 'techie' background. She was watching a BBC news story on CPDN which gave the web address at the end, and after prevaricating for a weekend, she went on and downloaded the software. It worked! She felt a sense of accomplishment and stuck at it. After a while, when looking around the website of the project, she clicked on the forum and was fascinated to discover the ongoing conversations. But she noted that they were all very 'techie'. She did not understand what they were talking about but kept going on and reading, and gradually they started to make sense to her. But she thought they were too serious so she decided she would contribute something to lighten things up somewhat. She went on to the cafe section and started posting. She was recruited when Carl noticed her contribution to a heated discussion on whether CPDN should join the BOINC platform.

Maureen, the now moderator, recalls: 'When it was announced the project was moving to BOINC, there was a lot of protest from CPDN volunteers. I wrote a poem about it and it was that I think that got me noticed'.

> What is BOINC? you may ask.
> Well, it can multitask.

A risky gambit?

DC – but not as we know it.

Share a platform with SETI!
Find ET, or the yeti.

CPDN's migration
will evoke admiration

and we can log on
thanks to D Anderson.

Picture the Pacific,
it will be terrific!

Trickles? What a shock!
Your computer won't stop.

Every day it will pee
just like you and like me.

Statistics so fast,
just forget all the past.

Collect cobblestones
for your patios and homes.

Servers so powerful –
all auto, no manual.

And uploads that fail
will no longer prevail.

Take us, Carl and Tolu –
We can love Berkeley too!

> http://climateprediction.net/board/viewtopic.php?f=15andt=2140andstart=15
> Posted August 5, 2004.

People responded very well and Christensen approached her to act as a moderator. He was consciously trying to assemble a team of moderators that brought a variety of 'value' to the project. He thought Maureen contributed to making the forum a pleasant place to be in, a congenial environment. Another moderator on CPDN is a professional programmer, so is 'brilliant' at dealing with programming queries. One moderator based in London is 'great with graphics, with using capacity of graphics for CPDN'. A moderator in Washington State has a 'farm' of 8 computers, and can build/assemble computers himself, so he has given indispensable advice on that front. A moderator based in Kansas is a professional meteorologist and contributes expert scientific responses to questions. A moderator who used to be very active but has semi-retired because of ill-health was renowned for writing accessible FAQs and anticipating questions.

The ability of moderators to communicate simply and clearly is crucial. Dave Anderson of SETI@home and BOINC notes: 'There's the conundrum where you have experts answering questions for beginners, the experts tend to use words that the beginners don't understand. And then the beginners get the impression that they need to be computer experts to do this whole thing so they think "to hell with it"'.

So Carl and CPDN consciously recruited people with a variety of talents to become moderators. This is one way the system administrator or PI, or, in the case of GIMPS, the founder of the Mersenne forum, invite people they think suitable and good for the project to consider becoming moderators.

In SETI@home, the selection of moderators is automated. Anybody who is contributing computing power above a certain level and who is also posting with a certain minimum frequency on the message boards has the opportunity to become a moderator and they are automatically notified. If they do become a moderator their term is one month to four months. There is no formal training but they have to read a list of rules, for instance, when is it okay to leave a message. If the message broke the rules then the moderators can delete it. They have to read the rules and understand them. As it is an automated system, Anderson notes that in some cases moderators are bad right from the beginning, but the other moderators tell them about that. Every moderator can see the decisions that the other moderators made.

For the most part, people who are moderators are committed and professional in their behaviour but not always. Anderson describes how

> we have had enormous problems. There's a phenomenon when you make someone a moderator, you're giving them what they view as tremendous power. They can delete other people's messages, they can even ban those people from posting at all. And the problem is the person who starts off being pretty reasonable gets corrupted by this power and ends up using it in capricious ways.

Super-Moderators

The need to moderate the moderators was one impetus for developing a category between the moderators and system administration and scientific team. The super-moderators are the most experienced moderators and serve as moderators to the moderators.

Super moderators are chosen because of the responsibility and self-policing they have demonstrated. Most projects have a private area of the forum, visible only to the super moderators, system administrators and scientists, where they flesh out debates on what is acceptable behaviour and dealing with issues that people running a project need to discuss. On the Mersenne Forum (attached to the GIMPS project), it is known as the David Hasselhoff room, an inside joke. One super moderator described the need for such a space as 'It's like running a school without a staff room, [you need] somewhere for the teachers to go and talk about what's going on, what's coming up, planning things, dealing with things'.

Vang of GIMPS says:

> We have nine of them right now and they have ultimate authority to do anything they want and of course I trust them 100 per cent, I don't worry about them doing anything bad. They're kind of like lieutenants, they go out there and chastise people for doing stuff if necessary. They are also incredibly intelligent people when they post. And when they post people listen and their names are in red.

When it comes to provocative behaviour, for example when dealing with extremists' views, it is possible to withdraw one's self from the discussion either by, as one moderator said 'using will power not to read it' or to make use of what Paul in GIMPS describes as the 'ignore sanction'. It is possible to tell the forum software 'I do not wish to read anything posted by this particular person'. That material then does not appear on your screen.

Repeat offenders of inappropriate or offensive texts are warned and if they do not stop they are banned. When it comes to banning people, that is usually dealt with by super-moderators. If someone becomes abusive the super-moderators can prevent them from posting. Paul, a super-moderator on GIMPS said:

> We tend normally to try and get some kind of consensus before banning any other member of the forum. A ban is enforced by the forum software which allows people to be banned from contributing but they can still log in and read what other people are doing but they cannot themselves post anything.

In one project, a long-running participant who is a professional scientist (a volunteer not part of the scientific team of the project) and a moderator, posted very good informative information but had also spent 'years beating up on people and yelling at them and generally being horrible. He tended to berate people who do not really know what they are doing' (super-moderator on the Mersenne forum). Finally, the system administrator decided enough was enough, they had put up with his bad behaviour because he brought productive science to the forum, but his behaviour was intolerable and upsetting a lot of people and he had to be banned.

Chris, another super-moderator in GIMPS, recalls:

There was one chap called D who loved to come onto the forum, post completely irrelevant messages, linking off to videos and songs. He's been tolerated for a number of years and only recently has been put under permanent moderation – nothing is released to the public until it has been read by a human. He didn't respond very well, he stamped his little foot and cried, but we gave him a great deal of rope and warned him many times if he keeps this up he'll be banned. But rather than banning him, we've put him under permanent moderation. If he posts anything of relevance we make it available to the public.

These issues are usually handled by the system administrator and the super-moderators as the scientists in general have little to do with the forums. This is a source of annoyance if not outright indignation for the moderators, especially the super-moderators. Even though, or maybe because, the scientists have access to the super-moderators private forums, there are occasional outbursts of frustration at the lack of involvement from the scientists. M, a moderator on CPDN, said 'A postdoctoral fellow recently took over the Scientific Coordinator role and after a month he still hasn't posted on the forums'. C, another moderator on CPDN stated:

the computer scientists are pretty responsive when you know there's a problem with the system somewhere, we get a lot of response from them. The project scientists seem very reluctant to say something. Whether it's openly or just to the moderators…there's certainly been plenty of incidents where the moderators are getting fed up of not getting any information from the project scientists. And you know they have a digital fit in private, on the hidden part of the bulletin board. I'm sure they, you know at times we've thrown a fit and eventually it's actually forced them [the scientists] to get round to writing an update so I know they do hear about our fits.

Appreciation and Support

Given the importance of volunteers and moderators – the projects could not exist at all without volunteers, and projects do not thrive and grow without committed moderators – the common experience of a lack of support and appreciation from the scientific team is startling. As John, a volunteer on several projects states: 'you need someone to support it, like setting up a local football club you need a coach there every day for training or nobody is going to turn up, it just falls by the wayside'. Or as Charles, a moderator on CPDN puts it: 'We're always looking for more from them [the scientists]'.

Paul, a super-moderator in GIMPS notes: 'I have certainly seen some projects start up in a blaze of glory and then fizzle out days or weeks afterwards because nobody has shown any kind of or noticeable leadership, encouragement or any kind of ongoing support for those people who are helping'.

As a consequence, on some projects moderators do feel underappreciated. The core problem in the view of several of the moderators interviewed was the lack of involvement of the scientific team. Maureen in CPDN was invited to the Principal Investigator Myles Allen's inaugural professorial lecture, and was there among the big crowd.

> He talked about the "thankless" job moderators do, and mentioned me by name, said, "where are you Maureen? Put your hand up, and thanks to you and the moderators". So I felt appreciated. BUT, a big but, when it comes to the day to day working of the project, it is nearly impossible to get him to post on the forums.

CPDN in particular is constantly introducing new models of climate change and it is a big task to respond to volunteers' need for help.

C, a moderator on CPDN describes how:

> There were special new models which were announced in 2006. The BBC were told how they were going to predict the climate in 2060, 2080 and that model would take 160 climate, not real time, years, and they were the longest model we had. We then had 100s of people downloading these models and registering on the forum...There was one volunteer who after 2 and a half years, her computer had managed to process the first year, year 1 in the model, in 2 and a half real time years, and there were still 159 years to go! She was one of the more extreme cases. There is only so much computer time and server time you can spend in that situation. However, you can't have people make the effort and get no response, and if they do contact the forums, you have to help them until you can't help them anymore.

The moderators on CPDN praised the system administration teams, first Carl and Tolu, and then Andy and Jonathan, for working tirelessly to support the moderators and respond quickly to requests for help sent their way.

The involvement of the Principal Investigator and scientific team does affect the project. George Woltman, the founder of GIMPS, although not a professional scientist attached to an institution, is renowned for being constantly involved and responsive, which in the moderators opinion has been a key factor in the longevity and loyalty to the project.

Einstein@home has a PI, Bruce Allen, that posts very frequently on the boards. The project is one of the most popular in the world. Allen views the volunteers

> probably the same way as a performing artist views the audience, they're people without whom I can't play. A classical musician is probably playing as much for themselves or their peers as their audience but without being able to keep the audience involved, they can't get gigs. For me the volunteers are a very important set of people I intend to keep them interested and happy as they're more likely to keep their computers running Einstein@home.

Dave Anderson describes how on the websites they have different labels that can be attached to volunteers.

> Volunteer moderator, volunteer technical liaison, we come up with these little
> titles which appear next to their name on the notice board. That makes them
> feel, that gives them a warm and fuzzy feeling...I think it's very important to
> establish a personal relationship and acknowledge their efforts. Make them feel
> like they're actually part of the team.

Anderson notes that most of the moderators on BOINC are European and every year BOINC holds a workshop or conference in Europe which a good number of moderators attend.

The moderators and super-moderators themselves are supportive of each other, and display in interviews a strong sense of friendship and loyalty to each other. As one moderator put it: 'We're in the trenches together'.

Their commitment and enthusiasm can be extraordinary. CPDN held an open day in the UK and moderators and volunteers were invited. One moderator travelled at his own cost, overland from Poland, sleeping on someone's floor, for a two day event. Bruce Allen of Einstein@home had a moderator come from Australia for an event in Europe.

Language Volunteers and Beta Testers

The text on all the different project sites on BOINC is set up so that it can be translated into languages other than English and there is a community of approximately one hundred people doing that. Having languages other than English has a big impact. As Anderson says: 'I know for sure if you want to get the Chinese to do something the interface had better be entirely in Chinese'.

BOINC has set up a system of support using Skype with multiple languages a key component of the new system. People can sign up to be customer support volunteers, put in their Skype ID and state what language(s) that they speak. There is also a web page that people can go to for technical help where they click on the language that they speak and they see a list of volunteers that are available to provide help in that language. They can see which of them are currently online with Skype and they can call them on Skype. Anderson explains:

> The idea is that when you have a conversation with somebody like a live back
> and forth conversation you can very quickly figure out what terminology they
> use what words they understand or don't understand. A simple problem, you
> know a typical problem can usually be diagnosed in about ten seconds.

Another group of volunteers are beta testers; they test the software when a new version of the BOINC client is developed, making sure that it actually runs on all the different kinds of computers in the world and checking for any glitches. Anderson describes how 'a group of about two hundred people set up a system where they can look, they do a bunch of tests and they report the results through a web interface. Only when we get sufficient positive results do we release them to the public'.

To conclude, software alone is not enough. Skilful community managers, system administrators, and moderators are needed to encourage collaboration and promote the cooperation and trust needed for a successful community.

The technologies, organization and power hierarchies make certain outcomes possible and others less possible. The flatter, more horizontal ethos driving volunteers comes up against their organizational position which can be described both as part of a network but also part of a hierarchy. The VDC project is a network unit itself but is meshed with the hierarchical scientific institutions which are the official homes of the projects.

Chapter 7
Principal Investigators and the Scientific Team

The scientists using the software don't want the user they want the computer... and they have to pacify the people who are giving them the computer power (John, VDC volunteer).

This is the unfortunate, and not inaccurate, impression that the average VDC volunteer has of the scientists at the top of the pyramid. But what of the scientists themselves? How do they view VDC? And the volunteers who are involved in VDC, what does it mean to them? Do they see themselves as scientists? There is a lot of resistance to VDC from within establishment science. Principal Investigators (lead scientists) I interviewed said that they feel VDC applications for funding are given low priority and that the established adjudication procedure of peer review of scientists within the established institutions of science, mostly do not grasp the potential of VDC or the role it can play in scientific research. None of the PIs felt that VDC was going to replace existing structures but there was a feeling that it had a place which as of yet has not been given proper recognition or support. There is significant fear of 'letting the masses in' and a mistaken perception that it would mean less control over the process, with fears around security. Certainly people are less predictable than the supercomputer cluster but not all research projects are suited to VDC so there is a selection process and secondly, those that are, have developed strict procedures to prevent fraud.

The science teams at the head of the projects comprise a Principal Investigator, usually a senior scientist capable of successful application for public money to fund the science, one or more junior science faculty, one or more postdoctoral fellows and maybe one or more PhD students. The head of GIMPS is not a scientist who is attached to a university but is a computer scientist who has worked in academia and the private sector. The PIs who were singled out by volunteers as exceptionally good – and each of their projects is very successful in recruiting and retaining volunteers – are Bruce Allen of Einstein@home, Vijay Pande of Folding@home and George Woltman of GIMPS. The scientific team at ClimatePrediction.Net (CPDN) were singled out by moderators as being less than exemplary by their volunteers, displaying a lack of understanding of the importance of their leadership for the project community beyond their scientific expertise. Projects which are way down the list on BOINC have one common factor – a PI with low presence, engagement and lack of transparency.

So what is it that the scientific team does, in particular the PIs, that can make such a difference to a project and to be evaluated in such different ways by the volunteers on their projects?

Their main role is that of leadership of the project, but leadership of a VDC is outside the traditional professional sphere of a career scientist, operating as they do mostly in hierarchical organizations – universities – with well established roles, rules, chains of command and routes for communication. Everyone knows what their position entails and behaves accordingly, including the leaders, the most senior scientists. They typically work with small teams, each member of which has a specific role and route through the hierarchy, of which everyone is aware.

Although VDCs have an element of hierarchy – the pyramid of scientists, system administrators and volunteers – they are much more like network organizations – a number of actors coming together for a particular goal, with many stopping once that goal has been reached, and certainly having none of the longevity of universities. They are also communities. There are some roles and some rules, but participation is entirely voluntary. What kind of leadership is required in this kind of collectivity?

Leadership in VDCs requires a range of qualities that are not always necessary in traditional organizational structures. Foremost is the 'ability to induce cooperation in others' (Fligstein, 2001) to keep the VDC project alive and ideally to thrive. Four qualities must be produced: a sense of trust in the project, identification with the project and the other people involved, good communications, and collective problem-solving abilities (Holohan, 2005).

Their degree of success in generating these qualities greatly influenced what Ganz (2000) calls the 'strategic capacity' of their leadership, i.e. the extent to which they gain access to salient information about the environment of the project, the world of volunteers, and the heuristic use they made of this information. Strategic capacity is greater if a leadership team includes insiders and outsiders: scientists and non-scientists, i.e. computer programmers and moderators/super-moderators are taken on board as key members of the team. It is also critical for the scientific lead to conduct regular, open, authoritative deliberation, draw resources from multiple constituencies of volunteers and root accountability in those constituencies.

Principal Investigators are also in effect leaders of the community of volunteers in any VDC project. The challenge for community leaders is to explore and treat the underlying needs of the community's members (Preece, 2002). Community leaders play an important role in developing the necessary social climate to generate community participation. Securing or developing such effective leadership is likely to be a critical success factor for the sustainability of any virtual community.

Trust and Responsiveness

A key part of generating trust is responsiveness, and the PIs who are responsive engendered tremendous loyalty from the volunteers.

George Woltman at GIMPS is known to respond promptly to questions, suggestions for improvement and to provide prompt solutions to any problems.

This has contributed in large measure to the large and loyal participant base the project has developed despite the lack of any institutional support. From the start, the responsiveness of Woltman combined with the topic of the project produced loyalty and longevity among the volunteers. For Woltman, he did not need to recruit key participants – they presented themselves. So now the physical hosting of the project, the actual server, is done by Scott in San Diego. Woltman recalls: 'He came on board in 1998, up until then I did it all by email. He volunteered to run a server which would do it all automatically'. Then Mike Vang volunteered to set up a forum which has become the very successful Mersenne Forum, and Vang bears the costs and does the work of hosting the forum. He followed a similar responsive approach, fostering loyalty and longevity over high achieving credit chasers or work unit crunchers.

A moderator on GIMPS stated:

> GIMPS George Woltman is a singular man in this respect. Easily accessible by any and all who want to talk to him, he listens to the needs of his crunchers. He continually seeks to optimize the client's code, often rewriting it completely for every new instruction set that is released. If a bug is found then it is fixed. If you have a suggestion then he will listen. He just plain takes the time and effort.

Participants can become disillusioned by the amount of support being provided by and/or the responsiveness of the project managers and switch to another project where their 'needs' are better met. This was evidenced in the large number of participants that left the SETI@home project in early 2001 when the network connection to the server that assigned work to participants was overloaded resulting in participants' computers being idle for long periods of time (Holohan and Garg, 2005).

Communication

An inadequate communication infrastructure increases communication costs for members and constrains community activities. The diversity of technologies and user skills among members further complicate such challenges.

The scientific team 'own' the project and are the experts on the substantive content of the project. However, more often than not they do not have computational expertise. They hire computer professionals themselves or use BOINC to host their project for free on the middleware it provides. However, the technical expertise provided by both these options is not enough to address all the technical queries and tasks in most projects and super-moderators, moderators and volunteers themselves fill the gap.

The scientists are ultimately responsible for the project and are the leaders in that if they exit, the project ends. This is not so with any of the volunteers or moderators, as there is always potentially someone else to step in and fill the gap.

They are also leaders in that many of the questions that volunteers have are to do with the scientific content of the project and can only be answered by a member of the science team. The scientists are the ones with the knowledge of how the project is progressing and are the only ones who can ensure that information and content is passed on to the volunteers. They are the 'gatekeepers' to information about the project. But what kind of information and how much should they pass on? The scientists need to know their project and volunteers in order to know what communications are needed and how to facilitate communications. The better one's information about a domain within which one is working, the better the 'local knowledge', the more likely one is to know how to deal effectively with problems that arise within that domain. Since environments change in response to actors' initiatives, regular feedback is crucial to evaluate responses to initiatives (Zaltman, Duncan and Holbeck, 1973).

David Anderson of BOINC, who is familiar with many projects states:

> It [communication with and appreciation of volunteers] varies widely among the different projects am ah, some of the projects, a lot of the projects have reached a point where everything is working well and they just view it as a utility. And like you say they never communicate with the volunteers. I think that's definitely not a good thing to do, these projects will eventually see their volunteer base erode. The other projects, particularly Einstein@home, is one that really pays attention to its public interface. And the PI of that, his name is Bruce Allen, posts on a regular basis. Some projects need it, others don't. Allen and his team regularly post messages in which they describe what they've discovered in their publications and so forth. And they also list the names of all the volunteers whose computing went into those discoveries. They do a very good job of not only keeping the volunteers informed but also acknowledging their efforts.

As Bruce Allen puts it: 'I depend on these people, I want to know who they are...' There are photos of volunteers on the home page of Einstein@home and Certificates of Discovery are sent out to the 47 people (as of end 2012) who have made discoveries of pulsars through participating on Einstein@home.

To know the environment requires commitment in time and energy. But a traditional, hierarchical concept of leadership will not necessarily see such 'local knowledge' as relevant and working habits will flow from this (Zaltman, Duncan and Holbeck, 1973). Hence CPDN's scientific team's tendency to provide a lack of feedback in the forums. CPDN does post information and content about the progress of the project but pressure from the system administrators and the moderators was crucial in getting this – the initiative was taken from below and had to be pressed home to produce results.

Network theory emphasizes that teams that combine 'strong' and 'weak' ties will have greater strategic capacity than those who do not. Leaders with 'strong' ties to constituencies are more likely to possess salient information about where to find resources, whom to recruit, what tactics to use, and how to encourage these constituencies to identify with the project (Morris, 1984). The ability to do this and to make this claim is critically dependent on the PIs' willingness to take on the more administrative and daily tasks of responding to routine questions.

The Story/Narrative and Identification with the Project

Hierarchical, bureaucratic organizations have clearly defined goals and programs of steps to get there. Network organizations, comprising diverse organizations, may not have these; network leadership is as much a function of framing a story or narrative to motivate people as it is implementing known steps in a programme. In terms of the leaderships' own motivation and the motivation of their team and network, the strength of their motivation was determined partly by the 'story' they told themselves about why they were doing VDC in the first place. The communication of such a 'story' or 'vision' is a powerful factor in motivating volunteers and maintaining loyalty.

Professor Vijay Pande at Folding@home likens himself to a 'proud father' of Folding@home and is a very visible leader of the project – literally, his photo or a video of him speaking is a feature of the About Us page of the project website. He has a blog <http://folding.typepad.com/> which is a science blog but pitched so a lay but knowledgeable audience can understand and covers a range of topics, some of them not scientific, related to the project. Like Allen, Pande explains everything, as he sees the community of volunteers as partners – on the project website, there is a section thanking volunteers and naming specific people as crucial in different areas. Professor Pande was interviewed by a volunteer and the audio and transcript were posted on the forum. The interview was based on a list of questions submitted to Pande earlier and ranged from general Folding topics to discussion of specific MacOS X (technical) questions. He grasps the interconnection, the importance of it and the opportunities that current developments present, saying:

> I think for decades one has dreamed about the use of computers to understand diseases and biology and to design drugs and actually for decades also people have sort of come up with methods which they hoped would be successful but really, it hasn't panned out as well as people would have liked, and I think it's only recently now that the algorithms are getting good enough and the computation power is big enough.

Science is a race to discovery also. Pande describes how the use of VDC puts them several years ahead of competing researchers due to the massive computational power it provides.

> We have a factor of a thousand times more power than most of our competitors in doing calculations, more raw computer power. And if you ask how many years of Moore's law would have you have to wait to get that, the answer is

about fifteen years. And so in a sense we can kind of do research that other groups could really only do fifteen years in the future.

Flexible Roles and Rules

The role of the Principal Investigator depends on the size of the project and changes over time, requiring a flexibility in approach and a willingness to share responsibility with others and accept solutions and improvements from non-scientists. Some of the projects are a one person show and the person in charge does everything. Einstein@home at this point now has enough people working on it, four people besides Allen, to allow Allen more flexibility in what he does. Allen says:

> My role is less. I used to be software engineer, system administrator, help on the hardware, these days I help decide what other people should be doing and pat them on the back for doing a good job. I try to make myself a point of contact for people who have made discoveries or played another important role, a job well done and get attention from the top.

Allen posts regularly on the message boards and says, 'You could spend hours every day on the message boards'. He liaises with the moderators,

> in cases that are obvious, they should respond. Occasionally something comes along that's curious and difficult, and I ask them to kick it upstairs. Occasionally there's interesting technical stuff. One guy was trying to get in touch, it turns out he had analyzed the program and had figured out a substantially more efficient way of doing it. The guy's a genius, and it eventually came to my attention as he sent me a message on the boards.

George Woltman has worked closely with the volunteers from the start of GIMPS. When he began it there were no forums, and he started an email list answering the questions of those who had downloaded the software. 'Ten years on, I'm still involved. I still maintain the programme that everyone runs on their computer, keeping it optimized, making it sure it works on PC architecture that comes out'.

George Woltman says of the forums: 'Yes, I'm on there every day. I'm a moderator, I don't really do a lot of that, there's about 10 moderators now, to keep everyone in check. It's definitely part of my daily routine. I spend an hour or two on the forum every day. My interest is writing software, optimizing software, that's what I enjoy the most. I'd rather work on the software than do the forum stuff, but I do check in every day, it does keep one connected to like-minded individuals'.

Traditional hierarchies have established strategies and methods. As VDC has very little doctrine in the sense of established collaborative strategies and methods, an important component of leadership in the project was to come up with such doctrine or strategic routines and methods.

For Bruce Allen, this meant particular attention to the home page of the project. There are profiles of all volunteers on front page. He says:

> I spend hours looking at these things...I look at every new profile to screen out any obscene pictures. I look at every new profile and see if it is suitable for the project. It's touching. It makes you realize that people really do care about science. There's people from the most diverse backgrounds..they never had the opportunity...they're scientists at heart.

David Anderson of BOINC and Bruce Allen of Einstein@home organize face to face meetings as offline interaction helps virtual community members understand, trust, and identify with one another, providing a stronger base for online community activity (Fulk et al., 1990).

Appropriate Leadership for a Network Organization

Appropriate leadership of a network organization is an extremely important mechanism for establishing trust, creating a sense of identification with the project, facilitating information transfer and cooperation between the organizations. By examining how scientists handled issues of authority, of doctrine, of establishing linkages with other organizations, of communicating what the 'story' of the project is, the importance of leadership as a mechanism for promoting the institutional culture that facilitates cooperation is clear. Bureaucratic leadership is very limited in this environment and consequently is not appropriate. Actors like Bruce Allen and Vijay Pande, in their practice of leadership in this setting, are helping to establish the type of institutional culture appropriate for a VDC. A network institutional culture requires different personnel characteristics than a bureaucratic hierarchical institutional culture. But these characteristics can be discerned, cultivated and emulated, just as the qualities of leadership and management in traditional bureaucracies have been through most of the twentieth century. The firms in Silicon Valley and the new network economy demonstrate this. Network leadership is a type of organizational strategy and institutional culture that is now recognizable in the business world. It is not dependent on pioneering individuals such as Jeff Bezos or Larry Ellison – thousands of business people all over the world now emulate that organizational business culture. Those individuals – through their success – helped delineate what leadership and institutional characteristics are necessary for success in the new interconnected world of business (and any organizational field): flexibility, an emphasis on expertise not status, an emphasis on communication and information as increased in value through sharing it, and responsiveness.

As Krebs (2010) points out, it would be false to assume that volunteers give and do not expect anything back. While the reciprocation is not monetary, volunteer computing is nonetheless based on an exchange. This exchange needs to be acknowledged and valued as volunteers need occasional 'feel good' messages to keep from feeling that their donations are taken for granted. They want to see how much they contributed and what results were obtained thanks to their involvement. Communication with volunteers could be improved through newsletters, orientation, as well as progress and feedback reports. As my research discovered, communication is one essential element in a range of qualities need to 'induce cooperation in others' (Fligstein, 2001).

Chapter 8

Volunteers

Who are the rank and file volunteers, why do they do it, and how can a project continue to recruit and retain volunteers? To answer the last question, we need to pay close attention to the questions of who they are and why they do it. As we have seen already, there is a large diversity of motivations for volunteers, broadly falling into three categories: science, competition and community. These reflect age-old compulsions in human behaviour – the need to belong, and the need to play, and to feel one is contributing to one's broader community. VDC provides a new opportunity for people to play out these needs, in a way that has a large impact not only on the individuals involved but on the field of computationally heavy scientific research.

Motivations for Participating in Collaborative Projects

Previous research on motivations for involvement in collaborative technological or scientific projects on the Internet has focused almost exclusively on the Open Source Software (OSS) community. However, participants in the OSS communities do not form teams and there is no element of direct competition. As a result the research on OSS focuses only on the motivation of individual participants in a non-directly competitive environment.

There are illuminating similarities and differences between individual participants in the OSS movement and individual participants in VDC projects. In an OSS project, programmers write code voluntarily. The source code for software is made available for anyone to modify, improve or extend, on condition that any programmer will then share the resulting code and software with anyone who wishes to use it. OSS has been so successful that many important components of the Internet such as the Apache web server and the Mozilla Firefox web browser have been created through OSS projects. The seemingly counter-intuitive idea of programmers working for free in the highly competitive and commercial world of software and computing has been the subject of growing theorizing and analysis in recent years, in particular the issue of programmers' motivation. VDC is similarly driven by individuals using their resources – mostly computers, and time if they are active on teams or in the forums – in a voluntary capacity that advances scientific research.

Although OSS contributors have not been thought of as volunteers in the literature, Krebs (2010) argues that is what they and those involved in VDC are. They are volunteers who are effectively acting as cybervolunteers, meaning volunteers who, in part or entirety, use a computer or the Internet for their volunteer activity. Ismael Pena-Lopez (2005) defined an online volunteer as someone who volunteers through the Internet and is physically located elsewhere than the beneficiaries of his or her actions.

Research on motivation in OSS has posited that how creative a person feels when working on the project is the strongest and most pervasive driver (Lakhani and Wolf, 2003), basic participation in VDC requires no extra computer knowledge. Participants in teams and forums figure out ways to speed up and expand the capability of their computer resources, and that does require considerable levels of technical comfort and knowledge to participate in many of the teams and forums. Overall though, participating in VDC is nowhere near as creative as being involved in OSS and the technical expertise required is much less than that in OSS.

A cost-benefit analysis approach posits that motivation stems from immediate and delayed payoffs associated with participation (many people are involved in OSS as part of their job) and the user need for particular software (Von Hippel, 2001). The motivation stemming from practical benefits to users of having good software, enhanced reputation from being associated with a successful project, and potential for OSS projects to lead to further commercial opportunities has also been forcefully argued (Lerner and Tirole, 2000, 2002). However, the technical involvement in a VDC project will typically not have an impact on the everyday use of computer technology by the participant, and will not aid their chances for further commercial opportunities through being associated with a particular VDC project.

Economists, including Benkler (2002) have argued that the benefit of peer production in OSS is the reduction in transaction costs (Coase, 1988; Williamson, 1985), in particular the matching of human capital to projects in a way that is superior to that produced by price signals in the market. However, in VDC the matching that is required is not that of skill to task but of idle computing capacity to task: anyone who has a PC can participate.

The most relevant insights into the motivation of VDC participants can be gleaned from work done on OSS participation using Maslow's (1987) theory on motivation, which describes a hierarchy of needs that drive people, ranging from the satisfaction of physiological needs to the need for self-actualization. Hars and Ou (2001), looking at OSS participants, distinguished between intrinsic motivation and extrinsic motivation, with the former including the desire of feeling competent and self-determining. Another variant of intrinsic motivation is altruism, where a person seeks to increase the welfare of others. VDC participants provide something for others (processing data for scientific projects) at their own costs (time, energy, opportunity costs, use of PC resources), and therefore belong to this category. A variant of this internal motivation of altruism is what Hars and Ou (2001) label 'community identification'. Participants may identify themselves with the VDC project or team and align their goals with those of the community. They may treat other members of the community as their kin and thus be willing to do something beneficial for them.

Ideology has also been identified as playing a role in motivating OSS participants (Stewart and Gosain, 2006) and several interviewees stated that political considerations prompted their initial and ongoing involvement in VDC. Chris Walsall of GIMPS was initially involved in a project in the late 1990s, Distributed.net, that wanted to demonstrate that the then allowed encryption levels under US government policy were inadequate. They demonstrated that it was possible for individuals to break the encryption and cracked an RSA key after only 6 months of work. Walsall says: 'I wanted to show that levels of policy were inadequate for the times'. Others cited being motivated by the need for action on climate change, malaria and water shortages.

Fun was a motivator of user-generated content contribution such as Wikipedia (Nov, 2007) and Open-Source and this echoed the findings of my surveys and interviews as the intense interest in competition and teams has shown.

Nov et al. (2010) identified several motivations that could lead to a volunteer's participation in a public distributed computing project. These include

a. enjoyment of social or educational aspects of the project,
b. enhancement of one's reputation in some social group,
c. personal values associated with the project's goals or the way in which it is undertaken,
d. positive striving of the ego related to volunteering,
e. affiliation with a team,
f. length of tenure with the project.

Nov et al. (ibid.), found that team membership was positively correlated with contribution to a project, whereas length of tenure was negatively correlated. Motivations had little impact. However, as Korpela (2012) points out, it is difficult to interpret these results as causative, and it is difficult to draw conclusions about the independence of these factors or the means with which they were measured.

Overall, there is considerable diversity in the studies that have looked at the motivation of volunteers in VDC, as it is difficult to prove causation when there is typically more than one motivating factor and what motivates volunteers changes over time. Most of the research has been done by computer scientists who recognize that volunteers are critical to the success of VDC and are intrigued to figure out what motivates them and consequently to understand how best to recruit and retain volunteers.

There is a growing body of research being done by social scientists to contribute to our understanding of volunteers. They have found there are differences between volunteers in the amount of work they do. Darch and Carusi (2010) classify a small number (they estimate 10 per cent) as 'Super-Crunchers', who are proportionately big contributors, with over 10 per cent of credits awarded to just 0.2 per cent of volunteers. Their category of 'Super-Crunchers' form approximately 10 per cent of all active volunteers in ClimatePrediction.net and are characterized by the relatively large quantity of project data that they process on their own computers, often running BOINC on a number of computers simultaneously for many hours each day, sometimes 24 hours a day, and they had frequently adapted their computers to increase their computing capacity. They tended to restrict themselves to only a handful (usually between one and three) of VDC projects, which allows them to accumulate a high number of credits in specific projects (rather than spreading their computational resources, and hence credit scores, more thinly over a large number of projects). Holohan and Garg (2005) noted that participants who are part of a team are usually more 'productive' and more enthusiastic about the project they are involved in. In GIMPS, for instance, the top two teams each contributed about 4.5 per cent of the total project output. In SETI@home, 1.25 per cent of the results come from the top team (Holohan and Garg, ibid.). Daruch and Carusi (ibid.) identified another class of volunteers who have little or no contact with scientists or scientific institutions other than through ClimatePrediction.net. They comprise approximately 80 per cent of active volunteers within ClimatePrediction.net but less than a quarter of all credits are attributed to them. They are analogous to those who are interested in the substance of the project but who are not motivated by the competitive or gaming aspects.

Holohan and Garg (2005) reported that volunteers' choice of project varies considerably, from those who follow SETI for fun or for what they perceive as a realistic goal of finding extraterrestrial life or at least hope there could be. One respondent stated: 'I'm a firm believer that we can't be the only life in the galaxy. It would be awfully lonely if we were'. However, they found that a primary motivation was the opportunity to combine cooperation or collaboration with competition, what they called 'co-opetition'.

In the 2005 survey, 60 per cent of the respondents cited the scientific contributions being made by the project as a reason for participating in distributed computing and 23 per cent cited not wanting to waste resources by letting their computer run idle. Eleven per cent also mentioned 'being part of something bigger than oneself' as a reason for participating. A typical response that summarized the feelings of several participants was the following: 'It's enjoyable for most of the same reasons online gaming is enjoyable. Friendly competition between geographically separated people of similar mindedness...'

Another replied: 'It's fun to be a part of something much bigger than just me'. Their self-identity as 'techies' put their opposition to wastage of computer power, and the importance of monitoring hardware and network health and learning more about computers at the centre of their narrative for belonging to the collaborative network. Mobilizing people towards a goal of scientific advancement and doing things that establishment science is neglecting or not putting sufficient resources into 'fits' the self-representation of the respondents.

The 'unofficial' story – indicated by the often 'sheepish' framing of the primary factor that motivates them – is the competition for success in the statistics tables on the distributed computing websites. Forty per cent of the respondents said they do it for the statistics, for the thrill of seeing their name up on the leader-board, getting respect from the fellow techies. Almost all respondents cited the statistics,

Table 8.1   Why Participate? Reasons cited by participants for taking part in voluntary distributed computing

Reason cited for participating in distributed computing	Percentage of participants
Scientific research	60%
Not wanting to waste resources	23%
Statistics	40%
Friendly competition	14%
Social aspect (fun, camaraderie)	17%
Being part of something bigger than oneself	11%
Gain of technical knowledge	3%

the worthy cause factor, and their own and broader technological advancement in their 'story' of why they are involved in distributed computing. They are all facets of the same fluid 'techie' identity, as often respondents cited one reason for starting and another for staying on. In general, respondents decided to try out Voluntary Distributed Computing as there was nothing to lose. Soon they got addicted to the point of responding to the survey question of why they did distributed computing by asking in turn 'why not VDC?'

Table 8.1 summarizes the reasons listed for participating in Voluntary Distributed Computing. Many respondents gave more than one answer, which are all included.

In the 2010–11 survey and in the qualitative research, I look at who the volunteers are and their motivation to join VDC individually and to join and continue in teams and online forums. The volunteers are mature with the median age between 26 and 49, 98 per cent of respondents in the survey are male, and the vast majority are resident in north America or Europe.

Motivation was fuelled by the opportunity to connect with like minded people on projects that were meaningful, *and* the opportunity to compete with those same people to see who can crunch the most data and head the league tables in projects. For many people it was both these motivations, but every project has a sizeable number of people who are not interested in the competition aspect and a sizeable number of people who are not interested in the substantive nature of the project – it is simply one more opportunity to crunch more data to get further up the league tables.

The motivation of the volunteers is affected by the type of project. ClimatePrediction.Net (CPDN) attracts more of the volunteers who are motivated by the substance of the project. This can cause tensions within the project as the two motivations are not always compatible in terms of the agenda of the project and the virtual community. This tension is reflected across all projects but as

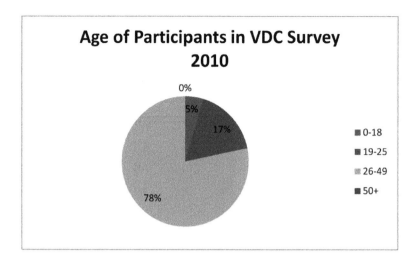

Figure 8.1   Age Distribution of Volunteers: Age distribution of
200 participants who responded to Voluntary Distributed
Computing Project Survey conducted in November
2010–February 2011

both motivations contribute to individuals contributing to success of the project, it does not necessarily undermine the project as a whole. In fact, it is a good example of the possibility of individuals and groups with diverse motivations, strongly held, to work together around a common goal – a feature of network organizations everywhere (Holohan, 2005).

However, the more prevalent motivation does have an impact on the fate of the project. Projects that are more driven by volunteers who are interested in the substance of the project are more likely to have longevity and loyalty from volunteers. Projects that attract more competitive data crunchers tend to burn brightly initially but fizzle out somewhat over the long term as the restless competitors' loyalty is not to the project or the scientific substance but to the goal of winning – and they will move on to other projects that offer more opportunity to do that or just because they get bored and want variety.

There is a steady stream of new recruits, and they come from all over the world. On one day in July 2012, Bruce Allen of Einstein@home, noted '103 people signed up for Einstein@home in the last 24 hours, 4 an hour, every 15 minutes'. He read out the origins of the most recent recruits to when we spoke: 'USA, USA, Canada, Germany, Canada, Turkey, Germany, Russia, UK, US, Germany, International, Hungary, South Korea, Italy, US, UK, US, Korea, International'.

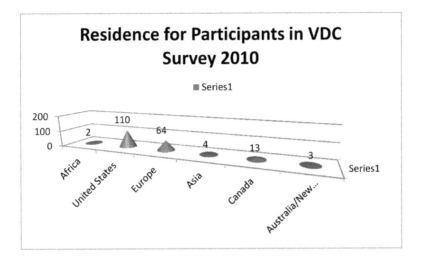

Figure 8.2 **Place of Residence of Volunteers: Distribution of place of residence for the 200 VDC participants who responded to Voluntary Distributed Computing Project Survey conducted in November 2010–February 2011**

Personal Journeys

Sometimes what motivates people online does not change, but their offline circumstances do. A volunteer and moderator on CPDN bought a business and that reduced his hours dramatically.

For many active volunteers, scientific research has been a distant endeavour about which they could do little beyond contributing taxes and hope some of it finds its way to research they care about. VDC changes that as volunteers contribute their time, learn and become engaged and feel like active participants in the research process. Personal experience and events that impact on a volunteer offline can be a powerful motivator for medical related research as evident in the following exchange.

On Folding@home, a longtime contributor posted the following, under the title 'Now, it's personal':

> I've been folding since 2002, determined to help the Pande Group do its research and support science in general. Now, the very disease for which I am folding has hit home. My Mom was recently diagnosed with Alzheimers. As you wish, AD, but this battle just got personal and I'm going to burn my rig to the ground crunching work units if that's what it takes to find a cure.

Several messages of support and empathy came through with replies such as 'Best of luck for your mom!...and have a look at these statistics Looks like the fight against Alzheimers is fought with GPUs, so use your money/energy accordingly'.

> I am truly sorry to hear that. Impressive that you've been here for so long! I wish you the best of luck with your mother and I hope to see your recruiting others into Folding@home *pushes throttle all the way forward*.

Volunteers do not exist only in cyberspace but obviously have real lives and events impact their interest and ability in participating in VDC. Just as offline, their participation in VDC can be characterized as a 'journey'.

In the 2010–11 survey, several respondents reflected on the changing nature of their participation in VDC.

> At first, I chose projects based on how beneficial the science was, such as curing cancer with grid.org. In time, as I became more knowledgeable, I moved on to smaller projects with better optimised clients, such as Find-A-Drug, which had similar aims to grid.org, but with software many times faster, and thus I considered it more worthy and less wasteful. Now however I mainly join projects for statistical and competitive purposes, i.e. trying to reach 100K credits in as many BOINC projects as possible. My reasons for doing this is that so many projects have seemingly similar aims and I can't choose one based on just the "nobleness" of the science anymore.

> [teams can become reason] I originally chose project based on what interested me personally. SETI was my first project and remained my only project for a number of years. I dabbled with a few other projects that came to my attention through my team affiliation, but remained primarily on SETI. After the completion of the stand alone SETI project and the release of BOINC, I was able to explore other projects, first Einstein and LHC, which were projects that interested me. I later became involved in the team aspect of DC which led me to a variety of projects, based on team recommendations.

> In two words, personal and convenience, respectively expanded: This is rather complicated. Initially it was self interested. I began with Folding@home in hopes to contribute to why defects occur in proteins as it may help contribute to a cure or treatment to a minor ailment that I suffer from and by contributing, I can help others as well as make use of the spare capacity of my computers as well as others whom I can convince to volunteer. it is a form of Pareto Optimality with great multiplier effects. In the end, I settled on simpler projects (Seventeen or Bust and Mersenne) as I found that folding at home interfered too much in resource sharing. When the software improves, I'll move back.

1) Is the goal obtainable. In the case of Seventeen or bust, there is a known quantity of data to evaluate, and hopefully all seventeen primes will be found. 2) Something that has a worthwhile goal. I also chose Folding@home because of its help with human protein. Again, I also feel it has "obtainable" goals. 3) I started out with SETI, but soon after moved on to the two above. I felt SETI was "looking for a needle in a haystack".

Mike Vang, who runs the Mersenne Forum, explains his own trajectory from credit chaser to relishing the substance and interaction on GIMPS.

> One of the things about DC projects is that people want instant results. Where things happens now. If you want a project to be successful you want a work unit to take less than a day. For a long time SETI had a screen saver version and when they switched to a command line version you'd get a work unit done in about 2 days or so. When I first started with GIMPS it'd take 6 months back then and it still takes a long period of time. One of the things working within GIMPS, working with these people…we seem to take a more relaxed approach to this. We're going to take our time and we're going to think things through. Now I'm like if it does take a few weeks or a few months or a year to figure something out, no big deal. Now if its personal progress or personal growth…I don't know…when I started DC projects my goal was to make money [credits]. At the beginning of the project I would have a very flush sites with lots of graphics and music and real easy to set up, switch a button and have work units pile up.

Prime Monster, [posted on 1 December 2003 at 18:36] a posted on the Mersenne Forum a document addressing 'Why People Participate in the GIMPS project'. He listed seven factors, some of which we have already covered, i.e. 'For the Glory' or competition; to learn more; to test the hardware; some particular to this project. And each project would have similar particular reasons.
He captured an element that underpins the quest for newness and discovery.

> Why do anything, why climb that rock, why read that book, why learn a new language, why build a machine? On the whole there are a lot of why do questions. And they can all, although not always, be answered with: For the challenge of doing it and because it can be done. Mankind seems to have this need to overcome challenges built into them from the start. We are always pushing borders and limits. I believe the answer to the question raised above, "if we lose the desire to do better, will we still be complete?" is no. We need the desire to do it, to overcome the challenge [Prime Monster, ibid.].

The technology at the project's centre is also a factor in retaining participants. A client – the program that does the processing – should be stable and well behaved (i.e. should not crash). Nor should it interfere with normal usage, and it must be easily deployable by the user on his or her home or office computer. VDC volunteers who are network or system administrators and receive permission from their employers for a company-wide or department-wide deployment bring in a much larger number of computers. Such participants need a project with special needs, which can be deployed en masse with very little human intervention. Technological factors are directly behind the most cited reasons for switching from one project to another. The most basic factors are the characteristics of the distributed computing program (client) itself: some prefer an unobtrusive client that does not appear on their computer screen at all whereas others prefer 'pretty' graphics. Yet others want clients that do not require too much memory or disk space or network usage. Still others prefer clients that do not require a constant Internet connection. Finally, many participants switch to a project they find more 'worthy' if the goals of the DC project are more appealing than the one in which they are currently participating. This is the chief reason cited by participants who switched from SETI@home to a project with medical goals such as the Stanford Folding@home project (Holohan and Garg, 2005).

Chapter 9
Conclusion

The more people that know about it, the more power it has (VDC volunteer).

Voluntary Distributed Computing is an instance in the transformation of the institution of science, catalyzed by information and communication technologies, and wrought by the individuals who are participating in it. It is happening in parallel to similar changes in the arts, in business, in all fields of human endeavour. Digitalization of information in all fields makes each of those fields accessible and open to manipulation by any networked individual, not just by the long established – and highly protected – institutions of science, or the arts or business. Anyone can be a producer and everyone has potentially something to contribute. Society is moving from an era of dominion of the industrial economy to an era more defined by the information economy. Networks have joined groups and hierarchies as social and organization models (Castells, 1996). The physical and capital barriers to entry of science, business, the arts, that were typical of the industrial economy are greatly reduced if not removed completely. The material means of information production is now available to networked individuals (i.e. individuals connected to the Internet) andthose networked individuals are making up an ever larger poportion of the world's population. If and when they collaborate and cooperate together, networked individuals can in effect establish a new mode of production, a social mode of production of information (Benkler, 2010) where individuals can produce, coordinate and disseminate information with no physical or capital barrier beyond access to a technological device (typically a PC or mobile phone) that is connected to the Internet.

This book has been a case study of the field of Voluntary Distributed Computing, which is characteristic of the new institutions emerging in the networked, information economy, and also is a compelling story of what networked individuals, harnessed together, can achieve. I have explored who the 'networked individuals' are that make it possible, and how it works in practice. The motivations of the individuals involved can be summarized as: science, community and competition. But for many volunteers, these are inextricably intertwined. To be able to participate in a community, play the game of competitive crunching and at the same time contribute to a worthy scientific project is a powerful combination made possible by the Internet. Different projects lend themselves to attracting and retaining a particular type of volunteers – although motivations are mixed, there is a polarizing tendency of individuals who are driven mainly by the excitement of competitive 'crunching' and do not particularly care which projects they are on, and those who are driven mainly by the science and do not particularly care how they are doing in the league tables. There is also a group who are driven by all three motivations, but in particular are involved, in a long term way, with a particular team or forum or community.

But this has also been a study of the individuals who are part of the proprietary strategies still dominant in scientific research – the scientists and programmers and funders of VDC – who are straddling the old industrial economy way of doing research and the new networked information economy of social production of information. VDC is a case-study of the networked individual, working outside the market, to produce information and knowledge that is as valuable as that produced by the traditional, proprietary state and industrial titans. In the industrial economy, the established institutions were the universities, the profession of science, and the state funded supercomputers they needed to do their research. These all still exist and are still centrally important, but the networked information economy has emerged to sit alongside it and both are now beginning to weave together in a myriad of ways. VDC is one example of this. VDC projects are still almost all based at established research institutions, professional scientists are still the only ones who can apply for state research funding and then lead the project, and the hardware (including the servers that host the project) is proprietary. The individual volunteers, the moderators, the supermoderators, the teams, the software and the information produced, however, are part of the networked information economy. The moderators and system administrators and to a lesser extent, scientists who understand the nature of VDC, are the bridges connecting the old hierarchies with the new networks, connecting the two worlds and the two modes of production. It is their investment of time and energy, their commitment, and their social skill of 'inducing cooperation in others' (Fligstein, 2001) that allows them to shape to quite a degree, how these projects are done. Their work is shaping one corner, the computationally heavy research corner, of the field of science. Just as it happened at the industrial revolution, the technologies are shaping – and radically broadening – contemporary organizational and institutional possibilities.

Future Prospects

The institutional possibilities raise opportunities to increase our understanding of pro-social behaviour, and to understand the implications of the shifting power distributions wrought by VDC and other collarborative projects undertaken by 'networked individuals'.

The networked information economy opens up new opportunities for community formation. Communities tied by bonds of affection, or in this case, interests and 'like-mindedness', are easier to establish and maintain and play a significant part of many people's social life. The connection felt can lead to and maintain commitment to the broader societal good, as in producing knowledge, including knowledge leading to cures for diseases, and the broad array of largely altruistic goals of the VDC projects. There are layers of connectedness and VDC uses the most immediate one, connection with communities of like-minded individuals, to support the broader community dedicated to the pursuit of a common good, most typically knowledge. Of course, such technological tools and the communal connections built on them can be used for goals that are not contributing to knowledge or the common good, as the tools provide the means for bringing to fruition motivations dedicated to regressive social goals as well as progressive ones. But the increasingly important role such connections and communities play in all fields means it is imperative to increase our understanding of recruitment and retention of individuals in any such endeavour. Close attention to VDC provides a case study which can cast light on the social processes and implications of the organizational and institutional possibilities being brought by the current technological changes.

From the research on VDC, it is apparent that communal ties typically increase individual productivity compared to those volunteers who are not part of a project community, and are an essential part of welcoming newcomers in and getting them successfully started. Projects with a very active and committed community based around teams and forums, increase their likelihood of longevity and inspire a very loyal, committed core which keeps projects going through the ebbs and flows of the larger public interest. Communities are also critically important for those volunteers who are motivated more strongly and explicitly by the goals of the project, where they get approbation for their motivation from 'like-minded people.'

The other central motivator, both in VDC, and in life generally, is competition, both against oneself and others. Being able to incorporate a competitive element into cooperative goal-oriented projects dramatically boosts productivity by individuals. In particular, it draws in young males who contribute intensively while engaged in the competitive element. Such volunteers however, typically do not stay many years in a project and move between projects as the conditions for scoring high in the productivity league shift. However, while they are involved, they are very productive crunchers of data. Many of the most enthusiastic crunchers form teams, and compete in this way. Participation in the project, and even more so in teams, inevitably, and as a valuable civic side product, produces a degree of 'enlightened self-interest' as the project unites players, despite any real-world differences of gender, ethnicity, class or political ideology, and reward those who are able to work toward a common end. Being part of a team unites the competitive and communal element most keenly, as recognition from peers overcomes feelings of insignificance that can be produced by being part of a project with up to one million volunteers. Achievement, publicly seen on the projects website league tables, gives a feeling of accomplishment, increasing self-esteem and self-efficacy, which further promotes involvement.

The software is critical for providing the means to connect volunteers to the project and to each other, but it is not enough. More experienced volunteers answer queries from new volunteers on the project forums, and these forums are in turn moderated by the most senior and motivated volunteers. This is a critical part of VDC projects as the scientific team typically comprises of the lead scientist and a handful of researchers and sometimes a paid systems administrator; they are completely unable to meet the hundreds if not thousands of technological queries received by the project on a daily basis. They are also reliant on the queries and responses for improving the software and developing the project. This is where the industrial economy model and the networked information economy rely on each other most visibly in VDC. This study increases our understanding of all the actors involved: the establishment scientific team, the individual volunteers, the volunteers who are active on the forums, the moderators and the super moderators, who moderate the moderators. The leadership necessary for steering a successful and long-lived VDC project is not in the scientists training and is actually counter to much of the leadership qualities which are successful within the research institutions. Again, this study contributes to our understanding of the leadership which is appropriate not just to a networked organization, but to the much more common scenario where organizations and institutions from the industrial economy are interdependent with a collective of networked individuals.

Notwithstanding the millions involved so far, the number of people participating in VDC compared to the number of users on the Internet is insignificantly small, so there is huge potential for more scientific research to be done in this way and for many more people to get involved. New projects can still grow without cannabilizing others (Beberg et al., 2009). There are millions of computers online in the world every day, most of which have idle cycles. If all of the computer resources worldwide can be shared to perform complicated computations for science, there will be a tremendous saving of time and money.

Grid or volunteer distributed computation is a proven alternative to an expensive supercomputer for doing parallel computation and some envision a global virtual environment for grid or voluntary distributed computation (Yao, 2006). Though voluntary distributed computation is still in the development stage, and most projects are still voluntary and experimental, it has developed very quickly and more and more scientists are working hard to improve its efficiency and security.

Besides security, which will become an increasingly serious issue, as VDC expands, the biggest challenge is how to recruit and retain volunteers.

On a practical level, with public awareness of concerns over the energy use of computers left on and their effects on electric bills and global warming, there is a very significant pressure towards projects that have direct scientific impact and measurable positive influence on the human condition.

Overall though, the barriers are very low, particularly for potential volunteers in industrialized societies. Nielsen (2011) points out that how far citizen science expands ultimately depends upon the imagination of scientists in coming up with clever new ways to connect with laypeople, ways that inspire them and help them make contributions they find meaningful. As we have seen, people are motivated primarily by their interest in science, connecting with like-minded people, and engaging in competitive, fun 'game-like' activity through the leader boards and teams. A minority have staying power, and connecting with like-minded people is the most important factor in keeping people involved. However, the majority active in VDC are relatively new and there is a huge turnover of volunteers. Notwithstanding that, the numbers involved are increasing all the time. So a key challenge is to understand why most people do not stay at it for a very long time so as to address this loss of contribution.

Bruce Allen, the lead scientist of Einstein@home, recognizes the problem.

> I'm very intrigued by the fact that if you look at the volunteer base of Einstein@ home, the vast majority is made up of people who join the project, contribute computer cycles for a few months, then lose interest and drift away. We're in a steady state, where the number of people entering the project about balances the number of people leaving it.

In 2012, the project hired a scientist, a postdoctoral fellow to follow a set of, say 100 volunteers from the time they first join the project long-term to try to understand why they lose interest and leave.

His hunch is, and the research for this book supports it, that it is human contact, whether through meeting like-minded people, or the competitive element, that keeps it going. Allen came to this realization through his experience on the project: 'When we adopted the BOINC infrastructure for Einstein@home, my original plan was to do it ourselves. I would never have thought of teams and credits, credits are monopoly money, why would anyone care about that? But people do'.

It has been suggested that since the exchange of textual information – a medium with low social presence – is still the dominant mode of communication in virtual communities, it is important for community developers to support community members with relevant graphical, textual and video interfaces (such as avatars, graphic images, and video chat) (KO 2007). However, current projects that elicit loyalty and longevity, such as GIMPS, have managed to do so with text based interaction, and David Anderson has described how there has been a very low take-up of the offer of the use of Skype among BOINC volunteers.

Paul, a moderator on GIMPS, does not see the high turnover of people as a problem, as long as a loyal core remains. He compares it to newspaper readership over a long period of time. He says:

> The *Times of London* has been going for something like 200 years. You can be pretty damn certain that the readership has changed substantially in that time. The fact that people have dropped out of reading the *Times* hasn't actually stopped the *Times* being a successful newspaper. You recruit new people. Successful distributed computational projects are set up in such a way that they are not dependent on anybody in particular, that they can progress with new people.

The issue of the capability of the volunteers to participate in science is one that is dismissed as not a problem both by authors studying 'citizen science' and the scientists and volunteers involved in VDC. Nielsen (2011) argues that most people are smart enough to make a contribution to science, and many of them are interested. All that has been lacking are tools, such as VDC, that help connect them to the scientific community in ways that let them make that contribution. In fact, currently VDC allows people to participate in science, but in a cognitively limited way.

Allen, reflecting Clay Shirkey's (ibid.) arguments about distributed intelligence, sees the future as tapping more than just people's willingness to use their PC's idle cycles. He explains:

> connectivity means everyone is much closer to each other in some sense. That's going to change science because of the following...someone told me that the soccer world cup final was watched by 2 billion people, so 2 billion people sat in front of the tv for three and a half hours, that's 6 billion hours of potential. They said imagine what you could do...my principle of 5 standard deviations.... you've got a group of people some of whom will have unusual thinking abilities. Imagine if you could get 6 billion hours of concentrated thought focused on some important problem, which would be the type of problem which a few individuals, talented in a particular way, could solve, but the average person couldn't, you could do amazing things. So...VDC is the start of something called Distributed Thinking. How do you take a problem you want to solve, say a cure for malaria, or a mathematical problem, how can you break that up into pieces, so the right piece lands in the right people's lap...you've got 2 billion people's attention for 3 hours..and so at the moment I don't see VDC and citizen science has really changed...I can't point to any breakthrough that could not have been achieved in conventional ways. On the other hand, because the world is getting increasingly networked, there has to be ways of taking advantage of taking this huge power of thought, and the first people or organizations or companies who figure out how to do that will accomplish remarkable things...VDC is a little movement in that right direction, a step in that direction.

The expansion of potential offered by VDC is equivalent to what Chris Anderson (2006) has called 'the long tail' of markets in the Internet era – the creation of many new small markets that are equivalent in value to the large mainstream marketplace. VDC allows for the creation of new niches of computational heavy scientific research that were not possible before and that enables the enlargement of, but does not abolish, the original and primary market for supercomputers. It allows for the creation of a new and related market or space for the social production of scientific information. This is a challenge for mainstream science as VDC is attracting scientists from mainstream universities (such as Stanford University and the University of California, Berkeley) and opening up computational heavy scientific research to the masses – or at least the many hundreds of thousands who are interested in participating. This is and will have a transformative effect on science as an institution. Already, junior scientists who could not have hoped to gain access to expensive supercomputers can continue with their research, thereby impacting their notoriously competitive career path and options. Research that would not be officially funded can keep going (like SETI's search for intelligent life in the universe). Basic scientific research can be advanced for much less cost and resources freed up for investment elsewhere in research (Stanford University's Folding@home project). The many who participate are engaged – science can be sexy again, as it was in the Apollo era, which inspired Dave Anderson to launch SETI@home.

But these are still relatively modest effects and those involved are impatient for VDC to realize its potential. From a practical point of view, the future of VDC could shift dramatically if one of two scenarios happened. Firstly, if a major scientific breakthrough, such as a cure for an illness or the discovery of intelligent life in space, was made through VDC. Or secondly, a suggestion by Bruce Allen and David Anderson – if the large companies (including Microsoft, Apple and Dell) agreed to make VDC a default setting, to put an app for BOINC into the operating system of every computer or iPhone they sell, the impact would be enormous, as the majority of computers in the world would be ready to go. Such speculation aside, one thing is clear. Voluntary Distributed Computing and the social processes it embodies are reflective and predictive of changes in production, distribution and the dissemination of information. They also, as I have shown, reflect and predict changes in the power of individuals and emerging institutions as they mature and interact with established institutions, forging new ways to achieve goals of all kinds.

Bibliography

Anderson, David. 2003. Public Computing: Reconnecting People to Science. Presented at the Conference on Shared Knowledge and the Web, Residencia de Estudiantes, Madrid, Spain, 17–19 November 2003. <https://boinc.berkeley.edu/madrid.html>.

Arquilla, J. and Ronfeldt, D. 2002. *Networks and Netwars: The Future of Terror, Crime, and Militancy.* Santa Monica, CA: RAND Corporation.

Barabási, A.-L. 2002. *Linked: The New Science of Networks.* Cambridge, MA: Perseus Publications.

Beberg, A.L., Ensign, D.L., Jayachandran, G., Khaliq, S. and Pande, V.S. 2009. 'Folding@home: Lessons From Eight Years of Volunteer Distributed Computing', Eighth IEEE International Workshop on High Performance Computational Biology. Proceedings of the 23rd IEEE International Parallel and Distributed Processing Symposium (IPDPS) 2009.

Beenen, G., Ling, K., Wang, X., Chang, K., Frankowski, D., Resnick, P., et al., 2004. Using social psychology to motivate contributions to online communities, in CSCW 04: Proceedings of the ACM Conference On Computer Supported Cooperative Work. New York: ACM Press.

Bennett, L. 2007. 'Changing Citizenship in the Digital Age', OECD/INDIRE Conference on Millennial Learners, Florence, 5–6 March 2007.

Benkler, Y. 2007. *The Wealth of Networks.* New Haven: Yale University Press.

Berger, B. 1960. *Working Class Suburb.* Berkeley: University of California Press.

Bourdieu, P. 1977. *Outline of a Theory of Practice.* Cambridge: Cambridge University Press.

Bourdieu, P. and Wacquant, L. 1992. *An Invitation to Reflexive Sociology.* Chicago, IL: University of Chicago Press.

Bruckman, A. 2006. 'A New Perspective on "Community" and its Implications for Computer-Mediated Communication Systems', in *Proceedings of the 2006 ACM SIGCHI Conference on Human Factors in Computing Systems, Extended Abstracts.* Montréal, Québec, 22–27 April, 2006: 616–21.

Burns, T. and Stalker, G.M. 1961. *The Management of Innovation.* London: Tavistock.

Burt, R. 1987. 'Social Contagion and Innovation: Cohesion and Structural Equivalence', *American Journal of Sociology* 92(6). May.

Burt, R. 1992. *Structural Holes.* Chicago: University of Chicago Press.

Caillois, R. 1961. *Man, Play and Games.* New York: Free Press of Glencoe, Inc.

Castells, M. 1996. *The Information Age: Economy, Society and Culture. Volume 1: The Rise of the Network Society.* Oxford: Blackwell.

Chatfield, T. 2010. *Fun, Inc. Why Play is the 21st Century's Most Serious Business*. Virgin Books: UK.

Chayko, M. 2002. *Connecting: How We Form Social Bonds and Communities in the Internet Age*. New York: State University of New York Press.

Christensen, C., Aina, T. and Stainforth, D. 2005. 'The Challenge of Volunteer Computing with Lengthy Climate Model Simulations', Proceedings of the First International Conference on e-Science and Grid Computing (e-Science '05).

Clary, E., Snyder, M., Ridge, R., Copeland, J., Stukas, A., Haugen, J., and Miene, P. 1998. 'Understanding and assessing the motivations of volunteers: A functional approach', *J. Personality and Social Psychology* 74: 1516–30.

Coase, R.H. 1937. The Nature of the Firm, *Economica*, 4: 386–405. DOI: 10.1111/j.1468–0335.1937.tb00002.x

Darch, P. and Carusi, A. 2010. 'Retaining Volunteers in volunteer computing projects', *Philosophical Transactions of The Royal Society*, 368: 4177–92.

DeKoven, B. 1978. *The Well-Played Game: A Player's Philosophy*. New York: Anchor Press.

De Tona, C. and Lentin, R. 2007. Overlapping Multi-centred Networking: Migrant Women's Diasporic Networks as Alternative Narratives of Globalisation, in *Performing Global Networks*, edited by K. Fricker and R. Lentin. Newcastle: Cambridge Scholastic Publishing.

DiMaggio, P., Hargittai, E., Russell Neuman, W. and Robinson, J.P. 2001. 'The Social Implications of the Internet', *Annual Review of Sociology* 27: 307–36.

Durkheim, E. 1893. *The Division of Labour in Society*. New York: Macmillan.

Durkheim, E. 1897. *Suicide*. Glencoe, IL: Free Press.

Engels, F. 1885 [1970]. *The Housing Question*. Moscow: Progress Publishers.

Fligstein, N. 1990. *The Transformation of Corporate Control*. Cambridge, MA: Harvard University Press.

Fligstein, N. 1985. 'The Spread of the Multidivisional Form Among Large Firms, 1919–1979', *American Sociological Review* 50(3), June 1985.

Fligstein, N. 2001. 'Social Skill and the Theory of Fields', *Sociological Theory*, 19(2): 105–25.

Fligstein, N. and McAdam, D. 2012. *A Theory of Fields*. New York: Oxford University Press.

Freeman, R., Weinstein, E., Marincola, E., Rosenbaum, J. and Solomon, F. 2001. 'Competition and Careers in Biosciences', *Science* 14 December 2001, 294 (5550): 2293–4. DOI: 10.1126/science.1067477.

Fullerton, T., Swain, C. and Hoffman, S. 2004. *Game Design Workshop: Designing, Prototyping and Playtesting Games*. Berkeley, CA: CMP Books.

Fulk, J., Schmitz, J. and Steinfield, C.A. 1990. 'Social influence model of technology use' in *Organizations and Communication Technology*, edited by J. Fulk and C. Steinfield. Newbury Park, CT: Sage Publications, 117–42,

Gans, H. 1962. *The Urban Villagers*. New York: Free Press.

Gans, H. 1967. *The Levittowners*. New York: Pantheon.

Ganz, M. 2000. 'Resources and resourcefulness: Strategic capacity in the unionization of California agriculture, 1959–1966', *American Journal of Sociology*, 105(4): 1003–62.

Geertz, C. 1977. *The Interpretation of Culture*. New York: Basic Books.

Gibson, W. 1995. *Neuromancer*. London: Harper Voyager.

Grant, G. 1969. *Technology and Empire: Perspectives on North America*. Toronto: Anansi.

Granovetter, M. 1973. 'The Strength of Weak Ties', *American Journal of Sociology* 78(6): 1360–80.

Granovetter, M. 1982. 'The Strength of Weak Ties: A Network Theory Revisited': in *Social Structure and Network Analysis*, edited by P. Marsden and N. Lin. Beverley Hills, CA: Sage, 105–30.

Granovetter, M. 1983. 'The Strength of Weak Ties: A Network Theory Revisited', *Sociological Theory* 1: 201–33.

Granovetter, M. 1985. 'Economic Action and Social Structure: The Problem of Embeddedness', *American Journal of Sociology* 91: 481–510.

Granovetter, M. 1995. *Getting a Job: A Study of Contacts and Careers*. Chicago: University of Chicago Press.

Hars, A. and Shaosong Ou. 2002. 'Working for Free? Motivations for Participating in Open-Source Projects', *International Journal of Electronic Commerce*. Spring, 6(3): 25–39.

Holohan, A. 2005. *Networks of Democracy: Lessons from Kosovo for Afghanistan, Iraq and Beyond*. Stanford, CA: Stanford University Press.

Holohan, A. and Garg, A. 2005. Collaboration Online: The Example of Distributed Computing, *Journal of Computer Mediated Communication* 10(4).

Holton, R. 2005. *Making Globalization*. New York: Palgrave Macmillan.

Huizinga, J. 1950[1938]. *Homo ludens: A Study of the Play-Element in Culture* [Translation of the original]. New York: Roy Publishers.

Ince, D. 2011. 'Systems Failure', *Times Higher Education*. 5 May 2011.

Jesper, Juul. 2005. *Half-Real: Video Games Between Real Rules and Fictional Worlds*. Cambridge, MA: MIT Press.

Keck, M. and Sikkink, K. 1998. *Activists Beyond Borders: Advocacy Networks in International Politics*. Ithaca, NY: Cornell University Press.

Klein, H.K. 1999. 'Tocqueville in Cyberspace: Using the Internet for Citizen Associations', *The Information Society* 15: 213–20.

Ko, J., Young-Gul, K., Butler, B. and Bock, G.-W. 2007. 'Encouraging Participation in Virtual Communities', *Communications of the ACM*, 50(2). Feb.

Korpela, E. 2012. Seti@home, BOINC, and Volunteer Distributed Computing [VDC], *Annual Review of Earth and Planetary Sciences*. 40: 69–87.

Kozinets, R.V. 2009. *Netnography: Doing Ethnographic Research Online*. Sage Publications Limited.

Krebs, V. 2010. 'Motivation of Cybervolunteers in an Applied Distributed Computing: MalariaControl.net as an example', *First Monday* 15(2) 1 Feb.

Lakhani, K.R. and Hippel, E.V. 2003. 'How open source software works: "Free" user to user assistance', *Research Policy* (Special Issue), 32(6): 923–43.

Lakhani, K.R. and Wolf, R.G. 2003. Why Hackers Do What They Do: Understanding Motivation and Effort in Free/Open Source Software Projects (September 2003). MIT Sloan Working Paper No. 4425–03. Available at SSRN: <http://ssrn.com/abstract=443040> or <http://dx.doi.org/10.2139/ssrn.443040>.

Lerner, J. and Tirole, J. 2002. 'Some simple economics of open source', *Journal of Industrial Economics* 50,(2): 197–234.

Levine, P. 2007. *The Future of Democracy*. Hanover, NH: Tufts University Press.

Locke, E.A. and Latham, G.P. 2002. Building a practically useful theory of goal setting and task motivation: A 35-year odyssey, *American Psychologist* 57(9): 705–17.

Martinson, B.C., Anderson, M.S. and de Vries, R. 2005. 'Scientists Behaving Badly', *Nature* 435: 737–8. 9 June.

Marx, K. 1852. 'The Eighteenth Brumaire of Louis Bonaparte': in *Karl Marx and Frederick Engels: Selected Works I*. Moscow: Foreign Language Publishing House, pp. 223–311.

Maslow, A.H. 1943. 'A Theory of Human Motivation', *Psychological Review* 50(4): 370–96. Retrieved from <http://psychclassics.yorku.ca/Maslow/motivation.htm>.

Mead, G.H. 1934. *Mind, Self and Society*. Chicago, IL: University of Chicago.

Metcalfe, R.M. and Boggs, D.R. 1976. 'Ethernet: distributed packet switching for local computer networks', *Communications of the ACM* 19(7): 395–404.

Meyer, J.W., Scott W.R. and Deal, T.E. 1981. 'Institutional and Technical Sources of Organizational Structure', in *Organization and the Human Services*, edited by H.D. Stein. Philadelphia: Temple University Press.

Mockus, A., Fielding, R.T. and Andersen, H. 2002. 'Two case studies of open source software development: Apache and Mozilla', *ACM Transactions on Software Engineering and Methodology*, 11(3): 309–46.

Morris, A.D. 1984. *Origins of the Civil Rights Movement: Black Communities Organizing for Change*. New York: Free Press.

Nardi, B. and Harris, J. 2006. 'Strangers and Friends: Collaborative Play in World of Warcraft'. Paper read at Computer Supported Cooperative Work, Banff, Alberta, Canada, 4–8 November.

Nielsen, M. 2011. *Reinventing Discovery*. Princeton, NJ: Princeton University Press.

Nisbet, R. 1962. *Community and Power*. New York: Oxford University Press.

Nov, O. 2007. 'What Motivates Wikipedians?', *Communications of the ACM*, 5(11).

Nov, O., Anderson, D. and Arazy, O. 2010. 'Volunteer Computing: A Model of the Factors Determining Contribution to Community-based Scientific Research', *Proceedings of the 19th International World Wide Web Conference* (WWW 2010), April: 741–50.

Organization For Economic Cooperation and Development. 2013. *Research and Development Statistics (rds)*. <www.oecd.org/sti/rds>.

Pena-Lopez, I. 2005. 'E-learning for Development: A model', *ICTlogy Working Paper Series*, No. 1. <http://ictlogy.net/20060713-e-learning-for-development-a-model-6000-downloads>.

Parsons, T. 1943. 'The Kinship System of the Contemporary United States', *American Anthropologist* 45(1): 22–38.

Pearce, C. 1997. *The Interactive Book: A Guide to the Interactive Revolution*. Indianapolis, IN: Macmillan Technical Publishing.

Pearce, C. and Artemesia. 2009. *Communities of Play*. Cambridge, MA: MIT Press.

Piore, M.J. and Sabel, C.F. 1984. *The Second Industrial Divide*. New York: Basic Books.

Porter, K.A and Powell, W.W. 2006. 'Networks and Organizations', in *The Sage Handbook of Organizational Studies*, edited by S. Clegg, C. Hardy, T. Lawrence, and W. Nord. London: Sage Publications, Inc., 776–99.

Powell, W.W. 1988. 'Institutional Effects on Organizational Structure and Performance', in *Institutional Patterns and Organizations*, edited by L. Zucker. Cambridge, MA: Ballinger.

Powell, W.W. 1990. 'Neither Market Nor Hierarchy: Network Forms of Organization', in Barry Straw and L.L. Cummings (eds), *Research in Organizational Behavior*. Greenwich, CT: JAI Press, 295–336.

Powell, W.L. and DiMaggio P. (eds), 1991. *The New Institutionalism in Organizational Analysis*. Chicago, IL: University of Chicago Press.

Preece, J. 2002. 'Supporting Community and Building Social Capital', *Communications of the ACM*, 45(4), April.

Putnam, R. 2000. *Bowling Alone: The Collapse and Revival of American Community*. London: Simon and Schuster.

Rainie, L. and Wellmam, B. 2012. *Networked: The New Social Operating System*. Cambridge, MA: MIT Press.

Raphael, C., Bachen, C., Lynn, K.-M., Baldwin-Philippi, J. and McKee, K.A. 2010. 'Games for Civic Learning: A Conceptual Framework and Agenda for Research and Design', *Games and Culture* 5: 199.

Redfield, R. 1947. 'The Folk Society', *American Journal of Sociology* 52(4): 293–308.

Rheingold, H. 2000. *The Virtual Community: Homesteading on the Electronic Frontier*. Cambridge, MA: MIT Press.

Roy, W. 1997. *Socializing Capital: The Rise of the Large Industrial Corporation in America*. Princeton, NJ: Princeton University Press.

Salen, K. and Zimmerman, E. 2004. *Rules of Play: Game Design Fundamentals*. Cambridge, MA: MIT Press.

Schechner, R. and Schuman, M. 1976. *Ritual, Play and Performance: Readings in the Social Sciences/Theater*. New York: Seabury Press.

Schulzke, M. 2011. 'How Games Support Associational Life: Using Tocqueville to Understand the Connection', *Games and Culture* 6(4): 354–72.

Shirkey, C. 2010. *Cognitive Surplus: Creativity and Generosity in a Connected Age*. New York: Penguin.

Slater, P. 1970. *The Pursuit of Loneliness*. Boston, MA: Beacon Press.

Stein, M. 1960. *The Eclipse of Community*. Princeton, NJ: Princeton University Press.

Stewart, K. and Gosain, S. 2006. 'The Impact of Ideology on Effectiveness in Open Source Software Development Teams', *MIS Quarterly* 30(2): 291–314.

Suits, B. 1967. 'What is a Game?', *Philosophy of Science* 34(2): 148–56.

Suits, B. 1978. *The Grasshopper: Games, Life and Utopia*. Toronto: University of Toronto Press.

Sutton-Smith, B. 1981. *A History of Children's Play: New Zealand, 1840–1950*. Philadelphia, PA: University of Pennsylvania Press.

Sutton-Smith, B. 1997. *The Ambiguity of Play*. Cambridge, MA: Harvard University Press.

Taylor, T.L. 2006. *Play Between Worlds: Exploring Online Game Culture*. Cambridge, MA: MIT Press.

Tapscott, D. and Williams, A. 2007. *Wikinomics: How Mass Collaboration Changes Everything*. London: Atlantic Books.

Tocqueville, A. de. 2007. *Democracy in America*. New York: W.W. Norton & Company.

Toth, D., Mayer, R. and Nichols, W. 2011. Increasing Participation in Volunteer Computing, in Parallel and Distributed Processing Workshops and PhD Forum (IPDPSW), 2011 IEEE International Symposium, 1878–82.

Tönnies, F. 1887 [1955]. *Community and Organization*. London: Routledge and Kegan Paul.

Turner, V.W. 1982. *From Ritual to Theater: The Human Seriousness of Play*. New York: Performing Arts Journal Publications.

Von Hippel, E. 2001.'Learning from open-source software', *MIT Sloan Management Review* 42(4): 82–6.

Von Hippel, E. 1988. *The Sources of Innovation*. New York: Oxford University Press.

Walther, J.B. 1995. 'Relational aspects of computer-mediated communication: Experimental observations over time', *Organizational Science* 6(2): 186–203.

Watts, D. 2004. *Six Degrees: The Science of a Connected Age*. New York: W.W. Norton.

Weber, M. 1946. *From Max Weber: Essays in Sociology*. New York: Oxford University Press.

Weber, M. 1947. *The Theory of Social and Economic Organization*. [A.M. Henderson and T. Parsons, Trans]. New York: Free Press.

Weber, M. 1958. *The City*. Glencoe, IL: Free Press.

Weber, S. 2004. *The Success of Open Source*. Cambridge: Harvard University Press.

Wellman, B. 1999 (ed.) *Networks In The Global Village: Life In Contemporary Communities*. Boulder, CO: Westview Press.

Wellman, B. and Gulia, M. 1999. 'Net Surfers Don't Ride Alone: Virtual Community as Community', in *Networks in the Global Village,* edited by B. Wellman. Boulder, CO: Westview Press.

Williamson, O. 1975. *Markets and Hierarchies*. New York: Free Press.

Williamson, O. 1994. 'Transaction Costs Economics and Organization Theory', in *The Handbook of Economic Sociology*, edited by N.J. Smelser and R. Swedberg. Princeton, NJ: Princeton University Press/Russell Sage Foundation.

Yao, C.-H. 2006. 'Grid Computation – The Fastest Supercomputer in the World', in *CSA Discovery Guides* <http://www.csa.com/discoveryguides/discoveryguides-main.php>.

Zaltman, G., Duncan, R. and Holbeck, J. 1973. *Innovations and Organizations*. New York: John Wiley and Sons.

Zerubavel, E. 1993. *The Fine Line: Making Distinctions in Everyday Life*. Chicago, IL: University of Chicago Press.

Zucker, L. 1977. 'The Role of Institutionalization in Cultural Persistence', *American Sociology Review* 42: 726–43.

Zucker, L. 1986. 'Production of trust: institutional sources of economic structure 1840 to 1920', *Research in Organizational Behavior* 8: 53–111.

Zucker, L. 1987. 'Institutional Theories of Organization', *Annual Review of Sociology* 13: 443–64.

Index

9 781138 271869